He Loves Me Not

By

Tanya R. Thompson

𝒢lory After the Rain Publishing House

This book or parts thereof may not be reproduced in any form, stored in a retrieval system, or transmitted in any form by any means- electronic, mechanical, photocopy, recording, or otherwise- without prior written permission of the publisher, except as provided by the United States copyright law.

Unless otherwise noted, all Scripture quotations are from the New International Version of the Bible. Old Testament © 1965, 1987 by the Zondervan Corporation. Used by Permission.

Scriptures quotations marked KJV are from the King James Version of the Bible.

Scriptures quotations marked NIV are from the New International Version of the Bible. © 1973, 1978, 1984, International Bible Society. Used by Permission.

Cover Design: Tanya R. Thompson

Contributing Writer: Mikayla Thompson

Lead Author Photograph: Mikayla Thompson

Editorial Services: 𝒢lory After the Rain Publishing House

gloryaftertherain@gmail.com

Copyright © 2019 Tanya R. Thompson ISBN: 9781790340552

Library of Congress Control Number: 2019915586

CONTENTS

Acknowledgments   i

1   Broken 1

2   In the Beginning 5

3   Prince Charming.................11

4   Tear Stained Pillow..............19

5   Words Hurt......................29

6   Guard Your Heart..........39

7   Love Doesn't Hurt *Introducing Ellie*....*51*

      Monsters in the dark....... 55

8   Who is This Woman? 65

9   He Loves Me Not 79

10   Domestic Violence Resources...... 91

11   Scriptures for Healing & Encouragement 127

12   Bonus Journal Pages.......135

ACKNOWLEDGMENTS

This book is dedicated to the vast number of women who struggle to continue in the silent struggle daily. I dedicate this book to those of you who go to sleep with fears and justified uncertainty pertaining to your situation each day. This fear is the by-product of a cycle that must be broken once and for all. I encourage you to hold on for just a little while longer. I want you to understand that you are not alone. We will break the silence together. Hold on. We are not victims. We are victorious through Christ Jesus. – *Tanya R. Thompson*

Chapter 1
ℬroken

𝒫urple. Red. Black. These are the three descriptive words that she uttered to the 911 dispatcher to describe the last recollection of what she saw as she received the devastating physical blow to her already withered, feeble body. Her vision has been hindered by the free-flowing blood that is running from her forehead. As she attempts to lift herself from the floor, a piece of glass that was once a part of a beautiful wedding goblet had sliced her finger quite deep. There was so much irony to this. A beautiful gift from the happiest day of her life with her now deceased husband, was now responsible for a horrendous injury on what would prove to be one of the darkest days of her life. The amount of blood loss as a result of her numerous physical injuries is unfathomable. These injuries would surely require countless stitches and painful surgical correction. She was just starting to heal from the last series of bruises and visible wounds on her arms and back.

In her head, she doesn't have the stable reasoning to realize that she will not have a choice but to take a ride in the ambulance to the hospital. She had been badly wounded before, but the severity of her injuries this time, were by far, the most brutal and intense. In her confusion, she wonders what the urgent care Physicians will say and will she even live long enough to make it to seek help? Prayerfully, it won't be as painful as the last time. The urgent care staff had become so familiar with her visits, that they would often times whisper amongst themselves at her arrival. The frequency of her visits had become greater as time passed. And, the severity of the injuries became even more gruesome.

The living room is a hopeless, bloody disaster zone. The amount of broken glass and blood-stained carpet looks strikingly similar to climactic scenes out of a criminal investigation program on a popular cable television series. Each time she tries to lift her head, all she can see are the purple spots dancing around her like little dragon flies. She is pulling herself through a sea of broken glass. Her elbows are too weak to hold the weight of her battered frame as she pulls herself to the stairs. The carpeted stair case was lined with the remnants of damaged picture frames that once held photos of happy memories. "Fourteen" she whispered quietly. This is the total number of stairs that she would have to somehow climb in order to make it to the "safety" of her bedroom. It was the closest room that had a sturdy lock. She knew that it took several minutes for paramedics to arrive. They had visited their address on numerous occasions. It was almost a rite of passage for the weekend. They were on a first name basis by this time.

The ringing in her ears is so loud that it is almost deafening. Her breathing is hurried and there is a harsh, crackling congestion strongly accompanying each inhalation of air. Every passing breath was more difficult than the last. The last three ribs are poking downward into her abdomen almost like a thorn in her side. She begins to ask herself if it is even worth trying to save herself from this monster. She placed her hand onto the handrail and used the last bit of strength in her body to pull herself up the seemingly insurmountable staircase. In painful desperation, her tears cry for peace and her soul cries out to God for help.

On each step that she mounted, there was a souvenir of the events that had taken place. On the first step, there was a broken figurine that her mother had given her as a gift when she moved out on her own for the very first time. She was holding her wounded rib cage tightly to ease the difficulty in breathing as she attempted to place her bent and broken body onto the second stair. She rested her head softly on the edge of the wall adjacent to the second stair. The congestion and blood curdling cough were becoming increasingly noticeable. There on the second stair she saw her broken key fob to her car. She slowly wiped the glass and plaster dust away from the surface. There was a large hole in the wall as a result of the previous struggle on the staircase. She leans her head back in exhaustion. She begins to weep uncontrollably. Her hands, face, legs and feet are covered with blood. Due to the length of the struggle, some wounds are beginning to clot while others are persistently bleeding freely.

As she peers out of her tired, sunken eyes over into the open-air living space, she notices that the once clean and crisp contemporary surroundings are now reduced to what appears to be a pretentious war zone. The wall to wall carpet looks as if it was the setting of a biblical time sacrifice. The beautifully arranged coffee table books are now broken at the spine, missing jacket covers and riddled with torn pages. The familiar artsy, rounded glass table that once served as the eye-catching centrepiece of the room, was subsequently used as a wrestling mat that would intensify the damage of her backwards fall. Her efforts to escape the vile hands of this monster were numerous and unsettling. This conversation piece is now reduced to a scattered disarray of broken glass chards and a bent metal frame. The beautiful custom designed living room furniture was once a place of retreat and relaxation. The level of destruction and chaos was far worse than the aftermath of the 2010 flood. Love could not possibly live here. It could never have resided in between these walls.

Questions torment and multiply in her mind. Why did she continue to lose herself at the hands of this abuser? Why not just give up the ghost? The one thing that kept her fighting this battle was her child. She knew that she had to be there for her precious daughter. She gave her a reason to live. Her daughter's loving spirit and kindness, despite their dire circumstances, gave her the strength to hold on. For this reason, she knew that giving up was not an option.

When dealing with an abuser, you must be aware of your surroundings at all costs. She realizes that the condo is brimming with an extremely eerie stillness. There are no signs of the abuser in sight. She seems to have lost all concept of time by this point. Had she been bleeding an hour? Two hours? How much time had passed since she had called 911? Why wasn't anyone coming to help her? She slowly moved her head so that she could fix her gaze onto her cell phone in her housecoat pocket. What were all of these buttons? She slowly lifted the cell phone to see if she could get a dial tone. Shades of purple, red and black flash as she muttered "Hello?" into the phone. Her mind and spirit seemed so broken and uncomprehensive, that it was not a phone, in fact, it was a remote control.

Suddenly, the floors rumbled, and the walls trembled. She heard a distorted jingle of metal with each boom. He was coming back. She laid empty and tired, still on the second step of the staircase, when she noticed the detached car key was inches away from her face. She inhaled sharply, as she knew she wouldn't make it to the third step. He burst through the door and locked his eyes on the key and snatched it. She looked at him frightened and pleaded with the last few breaths she had. "Please no…" He angrily drew his arm back and violently rammed his fist into her face. He stormed out of the door, leaving her there in a pool of her own blood and urine. She lost all bodily function, as well as her will to survive. Her entire world crumbled as her remaining vision faded to black. She never made it to the third stair.

Chapter 2
In the Beginning

Today was such a strikingly beautiful day. The birds were singing outside her window and the early morning air was crisp. She had a to-do list a mile long that needed to be completed in preparation for her upcoming summer vacation. She was a sophisticated, educated woman. She loved the Lord with her entire heart and soul. She took pride in her impeccable work ethic. This young lady saved tirelessly over the course of the last 8 months for this Island getaway. She strongly believed that if she worked hard and paid her tithes and offering unto God, that she was free to play just as hard as she worked! She was ready for some fun in the sun with her three long time girlfriends from school. They were planning to meet at the local mall to purchase items for their approaching international trip. This gave her a great reason to look for some new seasonal clothing bargains. In her honest opinion - it was always a good time to go shopping. Besides, she had just paid off her "like new" Range Rover. She had the title tucked safely in her safety deposit box at the local bank and the feeling of financial freedom was truly empowering.

This young lady was very business savvy when it came to her finances. She seemed to constantly plan for rainy days in the future, as well as the present life of her daughter. She was able to provide her with dance lessons, tutoring and private school. IRAs, stocks, bonds and residual income are words that are used openly and often around the dinner table to her young elementary school aged daughter. Truth be told, she is quite successful. Yet, she is equally as humble with her success. She is no stranger to honesty, hard work and calculated discipline.

Spending a few dollars on new outfits and accessories for her pending trip would be a fitting reward for her hard work. She pulled back her thick, white, billowy bed covers and placed her freshly moisturized, pedicured feet into her memory foam slippers. She shuffled across the hardwood floors of her beautifully decorated bedroom to reach her en'suite bathroom. She is wearing a beautiful pair of satin, lilac lounging pajamas. Fresh flowers are placed in a beautiful Waterford crystal vase upon her vanity counter. It had become a weekly ritual that she would go into her garden to clip fresh flowers. This is her way of living each day to the fullest. Taking out the time to smell fresh flowers was an intentional task that she was proud to complete. She was always determined to live in the moment.

She removes her satin lilac eye mask and immediately notices that her matching lilac, satin night scarf has fallen off as she slept peacefully in her bed. Her shoulder length, silky brown hair is carefully wrapped and pinned with precision in a neatly framed, circular pattern. There a few fly-away hairs standing ever so freely amidst the sturdy metal bobby pins. However, her longstanding Saturday hair appointment is happening later this morning. Thankfully, she can look forward to a refreshing deep conditioning treatment being applied to her long, flowing tresses.

Hair appointments were the highlight of her week and she looked forward to the much-needed time of laughter and relaxation. These hair appointments are quite special because it is their traditional mother and daughter time with one another. Her sweet, young daughter Ellie is accustomed to receiving the very same hair care regimen as her mother. Last night, she told Ellie to make sure that she placed her Kindle fire tablet on the charger so that she could watch movies and practice her sight words as they waited to receive their hair care services. Ellie said that she wanted to have curls put into her long ponytail this time. Her mom smiled and told her that she would have to sit very patiently under the big hair dryer. Ellie smiled and said in high pitched, innocent voice, "that's okay! I don't mind."

Ellie loved to climb up in the stylist's chair and sit down upon the booster that was added to make her tall enough for their stylist to reach. She loved to watch as other young ladies sitting across from her were getting their hair done as well. She would sometimes smile and wave at the other young ladies who were getting long beautiful braids, or intricately woven twists or even simple, timeless spiral curls.

Overall, this mother and daughter duo had built an extremely comfortable life for themselves. There was a solid reliable routine that the two of them followed and God was the centre of existence in their beautifully decorated home. Many friends and family members who came into their home frequently made mention of the peace and serenity that met them at the door. This home was filled with love, kindness and compassion to all who stepped over the threshold and into their humble abode. There were very rarely times that a harsh word was exchanged between these walls.

Breakfast was a very important bonding time for Ellie and her mother. It was an important time of fellowship where they talked about the day ahead and also prayed together before starting on their separate journey. It was a time of bonding and sometimes uncontrollable giggles and laughter. Their love was unconditional and pure. The rare beauty of their relationship was real. Ellie would often say "Nose to nose!", to which her mom would snuggle her nose close Ellie's. There was nothing of this world that could come between these two. They were two peas in a pod, Ellie and her mom.

Even though life was very good for Ellie and her mom, they had also experienced some extremely trying times. You see, several years ago, Ellie's father passed away in a horrible motorcycle accident. Ellie was too young to remember him. But her mother always shared loving memories of what a great husband and father he was. He was on the Deacon Board at the family church and everyone always spoke so very highly of him. At the time of his death, they were a happy loving family who placed God at the center of their residence. The home was filled with love for all who passed through the doors. There was so much to be thankful for. Life was good.

Ellie and her mother absolutely loved to pamper themselves. Nail spas were another one of their favourite places that they loved to frequent on a very regular basis. Her mother believed in the importance of allowing her daughter to be a young, innocent child for as long as possible. So, Ellie's mother would allow her to get her nails manicured and polished in nice clear or lighter pastel shades.

Ellie knew that between taking care of her cuticles and taking her delicious chewable gummy vitamins each day, she would also have long, healthy nails just like her mother.

Ellie would listen to the pleasant conversation that her mother held with the nail technicians each visit. They were on first name basis with the two of them. If you saw Ellie's mother, you could be certain that Ellie was not too far behind! Each time they entered the Nail Salon, Ellie's mother would take off her sunglasses and shout out "Hey beautiful ladies!" and all of the ladies in the salon would smile and reply to Ellie and her mother "Hey you two!!" Everyone would smile and hug. They would always ask about Ellie's school work and how dance classes were going. It was truly a special time for Ellie and her mom.

Ellie loved the feel of the warm water and sugar scrub on her tiny little toes. She watched as the water filled and the bubbles would rise. She placed her tiny hands over her bright smile and giggled quietly as Miss Lillian, (their long-time friend and nail technician), placed the wonderful smelling sugar scrub all along her little brown feet and legs. Then, Ellie would smile as Miss Lillian would vigorously scrub her heels and feet. Ellie loved to splash her feet in the bubbly, blue water. She loved the relaxing feeling of the warm towel wrapped around her little legs and feet. Miss Lillian would always bring an apple juice box to Ellie while she waited to get her toes painted. She would always lift her big brown eyes and tell Miss Lillian a sweet thank you. To which Miss Lillian would reply, "You are so welcome, Ellie jellybean." This was followed by uncontrollable giggles each time.

Mother & Daughter Lunch dates were another wonderful treat that Ellie and her mother shared. These absolutely delightful lunch dates were a time to talk about anything that Ellie desired to speak about. No topics were off limits. It also gave Ellie's mother a chance to help Ellie understand the importance of table etiquette and good manners. She taught her how to clean her area once she was finished with her meal. She explained to Ellie that this was a courtesy to the server. Ellie's mother had once explained that if she were at home, she would not leave a huge mess on the table, therefore Ellie's mother taught her the importance of being neat and tidy in public. She also taught the proper steps for placing an order and making sure to intentionally look the waiter in the eyes as she spoke to her. It was so important to give the utmost respect to everyone that they encountered.

Customarily, the lunch dates were usually followed by trips to local area attractions. Ellie's mother loved to expose her daughter to arts and culture so they would often frequent area museums and art galleries to learn about the world around them. This was a time to learn and explore about the world. Ellie's mother taught her that there was more to the world than her immediate environment. She encouraged her to continue practicing other languages and exploring various cultures so that she would understand how to embrace differences in culture, race, religion, sexual orientation or disabilities. Ellie's mother believed strongly that it was important to be an extension of Christ. This meant that Ellie should strive daily to live, walk and breath just as Jesus would.

Art was a major part of Ellie's world. Her mother encouraged her to draw, paint, make a mess and explore! Ellie's room was plastered with various works of art that her mother called "Her Little Masterpieces". She encouraged Ellie to add to her personal wall gallery as often as she liked. She would often draw scenes of the teachings she received in her weekly Sunday school classes. Ellie's mother was proud to say the least.

Ellie was thankful for a mother like hers. Their relationship was a very strong one and she knew that no one could ever come between she and her mother. Each night, as Ellie said her bedtime prayers, she would always thank God for her mother and all of the precious love that she gives to her. She always prayed for her mother's safety and protection. Life was good …and very good. For this, Ellie was thankful.

Chapter 3
Prince Charming

He was tall, dark and extremely handsome to say the very least. The crisp, precision edge up to his very obvious, already perfect hairline and beard looked as if he had stepped straight out of the barber's chair and into the pages of an editorial spread in a major magazine. The span of his strong, broad chest and muscular arms and shoulders gave off the visual essence of implied safety and protection. When he passed my girlfriends and I on the opposite escalator, the scent of Davidoff Cool Water cologne lingered ever so discretely as a gentle reminder that he was in the vicinity. "Good afternoon to you ladies", he said with his super thick, striking New York accent. His kind, soft spoken yet masculine nature could easily be considered every woman's dream.

This tall, fine specimen of a man had silky smooth, shapely, well moisturized lips. It appeared that they were well acquainted with Carmex. Those beautiful lips were the perfect accessory to his glistening white teeth; which (might I add) were super straight – free of spaces and appeared to be flossed no less than ten times daily. He could have easily been cast for the starring role of a popular toothpaste commercial. Those beautiful ivory tinted teeth laid nicely in the background against his clear, chocolatey smooth black skin. As we passed one another on the escalator in the local upscale shopping mall, I couldn't help but notice that the light was hitting his large diamond stud earrings just right. Between his award-winning teeth and his large glistening earrings, there was enough light radiating in a prism light fashion to fill the entire breezeway. His big, strong, masculine hands were holding several large shopping bags with ease. You could see the bulging veins in his strong forearms rising close to his chocolate covered skin. Child, I tell you what; he looked as fresh as the morning breeze in his starched, white Polo shirt and neatly pressed Hugo Boss jeans.

The slightest hint of his bow-legged silhouette was evidenced by the gently arched stance on the escalator steps. From head to toe, everything was fresh and crisp on this man; right down to the stark white shoestrings in his tennis shoes on his rather large feet. He was the sum total of what you might call; a beautiful sight to behold.

My girlfriends and I were headed up the escalator to browse Neiman Marcus for some trendy new clothing pieces for our upcoming International excursion. It was quite obvious that "Prince Charming" couldn't take his eyes off me the entire escalator ride. He was coming down on the opposite side as we were ascending up to the third floor. My girlfriends crowded around and smiled. I smiled radiantly and waved a hearty goodbye to "Prince Charming" as my girlfriends and I stepped gingerly off the escalator. Our attention quickly refocused as we walked right into the open-air, wondrous glory of Neiman Marcus. In the background, the smooth hum of the empty escalator played like an afternoon classical symphony. We never took a second thought about Prince Charming. You could rest assured that new clothing and accessories would surely be our reasonable portion.

It's 4:30 p.m. and my homegirls and I have shopped until we were ready to drop. We had left no stones unturned. By stones, I mean fabulous sales at each of our favorite boutiques. It is safe to say that we have completely shut the entire mall down! My girls are super pumped about our upcoming trip. It is so refreshing to be in the company of such smart, successful women. Each of us were at the top of our game and we were in desperate need of this girl's getaway shopping trip. It was so refreshing to be in the company of like-minded women. The conversations were never empty or one sided. There was always a sense of camaraderie amongst us.

The atmosphere was always celebratory for our personal successes. Rayna was celebrating the fact that she had just won her 12th consecutive case since passing her bar exam. She had put her law career on hold for several years so that she and her husband could raise their two twin girls named Lilly and Bria.

Bentley was a real estate mogul in her own right. We had lost count of the number of homes that she had sold to high profile clients this year. This sister was doing her thing. She met her husband Rodger, who is also a successful realtor on a celebrity open house tour. The Howell's were truly a real estate power couple. They didn't have children yet, but that didn't mean that they weren't trying.

Pamela and I were both Masters-Level prepared Nurses in the Government Research Program. We had just landed what was considered tenure status. If we played our cards correctly, we would be set for life. I was newly widowed. Pamela was single with no children. She had never married and did not seem to be searching. So, in the spirit of sisterhood and celebration; we came, we shopped, and we conquered!

We had come to the end of the day and our shopping bags were exponentially full and our stomachs were totally empty. We decided to go to our group's favorite dining spot, which was the Cheesecake Factory. This restaurant was like our boss lady headquarters for the group. We ordered our entrees and took our desserts out with us to enjoy at a later time. The hours went by as we laughed and talked about all of the exciting excursions that we were going to experience on our upcoming vacation get away. I looked at my watch and realized how late it was and that I had to get back home to my sweet, beloved Ellie. If I know my Ellie, she was probably waiting with the most endearing picture to give to me. Naturally, we got our desserts packaged to go and headed out to the parking lot together. Our motto was always to come together, stay together and leave together. No homegirl left behind. We meant that thing. My girls and I were thick as thieves. We could have easily had jackets made.

We spent a tremendous amount of time on the restaurant patio that day. We reminisced and laughed so long that we were the only 4 cars left in the side parking lot. I reached in my purse to look for my keys. Beyond the shopping receipts, my oversized makeup bag and my phone charger I did not readily feel my Rover key chain. I immediately panicked. Not because of the missing car keys. I was concerned about the missing keychain. This keychain was very sentimental to me. My late husband surprised me with the Range Rover for my 35th birthday. This keychain was dear to me. Even more so than the SUV. It was beautifully wrapped in a lovely green box and placed under the tree that Christmas. My mind ran back to when my excess walked Ellie and I out to the garage to see what the key belonged to. It would be our last Christmas with one another. I must admit that I started to panic. My girls circled around and used the flashlights on their cell phones to shine a bright light on the situation at hand. To our chagrin, the keys to the Rover were nowhere to be found. I pulled up the number to dial roadside assistance. I was praying that they could come out and cut another key on spot. Suddenly I hear a deep voice from the shadows say the words "Baby girl! Are you missing your keys?" His familiar bow-legged frame walked from behind the shadows holding my keys out beside his beautiful brown frame.

It was him. Hours had passed since we last saw him and he still looked as smooth as a morning breeze on a hot summer day. I was so taken back by his attractiveness that I found myself stammering and hard to get my words out. "Say something, girl" my friends whisper to me. "Y-yes! Those are mine." But then a lightbulb came on and I said sternly "Umm, how did you find them?" I said. To which he replied, "Well, judging by the olive color of your dress and juniper tint of your manicured nails, I figured this lovely chartreuse charm on these keys belonged to you, beautiful." He flashed those beautiful white teeth. I could hardly contain myself as I saw him examine the curves and contours of my physique. For good measure, I silently prayed, "Lord, help me to crucify my flesh right here where I stand." I was asking the Lord to save me from my own fleshly desires.

As I stood there stunned in silence, he added "Truth is, I saw you leave the Louis V Boutique and the sales floor associate was too late to catch you. I easily convinced them that I knew you. I figured that I would wait to see you and give them to you personally." (⏸) He grinned charmingly. I turned back to my girls and they gave me a suggestive smile with a mixture of confusion. He smiled and gave a smooth head nod as my girls popped their trunks simultaneously to place their packages inside. They continued to walk gingerly to their cars which were all parked on the same row. Prince Charming said "Goodnight, lovely queens. I am right here. I will make sure that you lovely ladies get to your cars safely." He leaned confidently and even arrogantly onto the driver's side door of my Range Rover. He leaned on it as if he *knew me*. And, he really thinks that my girls are about to leave me here with him? Alone. Yeah, ok. I know this negro doesn't think this is that type of game! If this book had a pause button, right here is where would freeze this whole scene and get some things straight! I need for you to fully understand the unbreakable bond that my girls and I shared. So, let me place "Prince Charming" on imaginary pause status momentarily and tell you about my A-1s since day one.

My homegirls are Bentley, Rayna and Pamela. We have known one another for a very long time. Bentley, Rayna and I have known one another since double-dutch on the school yard in 6th grade. We met Pamela our freshman year in High School trying out for the track team. All four of us were sprinters. The four of us trained together and ran the 100m, 200m and 400-meter relays. And, please believe, we set the track on fire at all costs. And yes ma'am we have the hardware to prove it. One of our greatest memories was capturing the State Championship title in the 400-meter relay. The four of us have been inseparable ever since. Our squad has had one another's backs down through the years without a doubt. We have seen one another wear plastic jelly shoes and clack balls in our ponytails. We have rocked charm necklaces and panda bear coin ring. We have laughed about wet collars from free flowing over moisturized Jheri curls. We were trendsetters in when we were the first ones to rock the asymmetrical Salt n' Pepa style haircuts. Even though, sweet Rayna lost most her hair when we tried to die her hair platinum…right after perming it! Yes, I know, not the brightest idea. We survived music from Menudo to Michael Jackson. I'm talking the *Off the Wall* album to *Thriller*. We listened to vinyl albums of Luther Vandross religiously. We loved all thigs Luther. It didn't matter what variation or from which era. From Big Luther to little Luther, we were committed to becoming his biggest fans. There were times when we danced to the smooth sounds of *Come and Talk to Me* by Jodeci. I remember very vividly the night that we all cried together during one of our weekend slumber parties because sweet Rayna's first break up had just happened. We listened to *You Don't Have to Hurt No More* by Mint Condition on repeat until the sun came up. I also remember standing in a circle with each of our High School sweethearts on Prom Night 1994 dancing to *Before I Let You Go* by Black Street. We watched shows like a Different World on Thursday evenings together, in preparation for going away to College. When we went away to Spelman, Howard and TSU even the hundreds of miles could not separate us. Pamela and I made our home away from home at Tennessee State University nursing students. Bentley was off to Spelman determined to become a Business major and sweet Rayna went away to Howard University to study Pre-Law. My homegirls and I have stood the test of time. Our bond was unbreakable. And, now let us venture back into our story. Pull out your imaginary pause button, press that bad boy and let's find out what my girls have to say.

Prince Charming is still leaning towards the side of my green whip (as my late husband called the Rover), so arrogantly. As he folded his arms, he released a gentle breeze of the Davidoff Cool Water cologne that unleashed a feeling of temptation to at least three of my five senses earlier in the day. Even, the irresistible scent of this cologne could not mask the terrible scent of arrogance and pride at this point. His arrogance was a complete turn off. I felt he was marking new territory. I was his prey.

Once my home girls placed their bags in their individual cars, they heard what Prince Charming said. It seemed that they simultaneously focused their attention on him. These women slowly turned in sync and all you could hear was the unison sounds of clacking stilettos moving rapidly towards the Rover. When they arrived at my car, I stepped forward and swiftly did a pivot turn on my Red Bottom heel to meet them in the midst of their cadence. We stood like a small army. All we needed was a drill sergeant to give us marching orders. We were giving this guy the "Oh, no you didn't" death stare. The four of us looked this joker up and down. Bentley began to roll her eyes and started loudly sucking her teeth until finally she belted out, "So you really think your just gonna lay all over her car door? Like you pay the note and rode here together? Negro, we don't know you!" Prince Charming smiled and drop his head to the side. As he grinned sheepishly, he smoothly jumped up and said "Oh, my bad." He took his hand and pretended to wipe off my door. He said in a low, deep voice "So, you like green, huh? Well, I like black. Black is always in style, its classic, timeless and you can always count on it to make you look your best." As he spoke, I was gazing into his eyes. Not out of flesh but more out of stubbornness. What was this man's motive?

I lifted my hand to reach for my keys and he smoothly grabbed my manicured hand. We continued to gaze into one another's eyes as he placed his smooth, chap stick lined lips onto my hand. Bentley stepped forward and Pamela stepped with her. Sweet Rayna, though soft spoken could also cut you long deep and wide if absolutely necessary. I spoke up and said ladies I think it's time to bid the gentleman goodnight. Prince Charming kept talking as if it were noon day on a Saturday. It was late, it was dark outside, and it was definitely time to head home to my Ellie.

At that moment, Bentley jumped into her car and rolled down the passenger side window to her tiny sports car. She began to beat on her car horn like Interstate 40 going west. Prince Charming was once like kryptonite, but his newly displayed arrogance was the perfect antidote. It was truly a turn off. However, he seemed to be determined to pursue the thought of obtaining "my digits." He was persistent. But, so was the long, abrasive sound of Bentley's high-pitched squeaking horn. Initially, I desperately needed to be brought back to reality. The tables turned and he was the one who needed a reality check. Pamela leaned across the seat of her two door BMW and yelled out, "Exchange the digits if you so desire, or count your losses. Let's roll!"

He stood with a straight face and reluctantly opened my door. I sarcastically thanked him and slid effortlessly onto my tan leather seats. The new car smell was a welcome reminder of the previous life I had built with my husband prior to his passing. It was familiar. I felt safe.

As I turned the key to my truck, I couldn't help but feel a sense of loneliness. I sat for a moment with both hands on the steering wheel as the engine purred quietly. As I thought about the amazing day that was behind me, I felt a sense of emptiness when I thought about returning home to that empty space in my bed that once belonged to my husband. I sighed and adjusted my rear-view mirror. Out of my side view mirror I noticed that Prince Charming was standing with his arms folded awaiting us to pull out of the parking lot. He smiled and motioned his hands into the shaped of a telephone. Those pearly white teeth were glistening as he awaited my answer in pantomime. I reached for my business card holder. I figured it would just be friendly conversation. I rolled down my window and handed him one of my business cards. He smiled and handed me his as well.

At that moment, I realized that I had not even ask his name. I looked down at the card. He looked at mine. We exchanged one last smile and went about our separate ways. By this time, my homegirls had pulled their cars out of their parking spaces and were sitting in formation! We rolled out of the parking lot in concert and headed towards our various destinations.

As I started driving towards my mother's house to pick up Ellie, I became overwhelmed with emotions. I missed my husband dearly. Things had not been the same since he was killed. The love that we shared was so real. We understood one another. We shared a life together. Our time of bereavement had no yet fully ended, I was not sure what the future would hold for Ellie and myself. But there was one thing certain. I knew that if we kept God in the center of our lives, He would never leave us nor forsake. That drive home was a long ride that night. I was ready to see the sun shine in my life again.

.

Bereavement – noun. a period of mourning after a loss, especially after the death of a loved one: a state of intense grief, as after the loss of a loved one; desolation; deprivation or loss by force. – *Merriam Webster*

Chapter 4
Tear Stained Pillow

Home at last. I slowly turned the house key and walked very quietly into our condominium foyer. The alternating, diamond-shaped, black and white patterned, marble tile echoed the familiar click-clacking symphony of my Red Bottom heels as I made my way across the sea of slippery marble and onto the soothing, thick white carpeted floors of the great room. Ellie's excitement had turned to a peaceful sleep on the ride home. I loved carrying her in my arms like the precious package that she was. I carefully slid my heels off while still holding Ellie in my arms. I gently laid my various shopping bags against the adjacent staircase. The alarm was located close to the great room behind a picture of hummingbirds. I reached out with my free arm to put in the alarm code to disarm the system. I looked up at the large, low hanging crystal chandelier and focused my vision on the second story overhanging loft and newly decorated guest bedroom. Lately, it seemed so lifeless and empty up there. I very seldom ascended the staircase to this wing of memories. I was still so very heartbroken. I truly missed my dear husband.

I gathered my thoughts and reminded myself that I must put Ellie to bed. She was such a beautiful reminder of the love that my husband and I once shared. As a by-product of our love, she came into existence. Despite my husband's untimely death, a part of him lives on through her. I smiled and gently kissed her on the forehead. I turned and continued our way to her bedroom. The fresh aroma of homemade potpourri tickled my nostrils as I moved down the foyer and past my husband's office. The familiar smell of freshly painted walls and new furniture served as a nostalgic reminder of the recent redecoration and repurposing of this space that served as my husband's man cave and office. This nostalgic fragrance in the form of new paint was the sad reminder that he would no longer grace these walls.

We made our way around the corner and into Ellie's bedroom. I was still standing in the doorway holding Ellie tightly in my arms. She was sleeping ever so peacefully, without a care in the world right there on my shoulder. I caught a fast glimpse of our mother-daughter portrait in motion which was reflecting from the large mirror across the hallway as we walked past. My long silky curls were like a sweet comforting shawl that cascaded down my shoulder and over onto Ellie's face. Her slightly dishevelled curls showed the signs of a playful day with grandma. Never the less, she and her curls were still just as beautiful as ever. I placed her on the bed for a few moments while I gathered my thoughts. I was so blessed to have a piece of my husband here with me. I could not have asked for a more beautiful expression of living love. I began to reflect on the day.

I was always so excited to be reunited with Ellie at my mother's house. The feeling was mutual when it came to our mother daughter relationship. Just as I had suspected earlier, it was confirmed that Ellie stayed up well past her bedtime in anticipation for my arrival as evidenced by her sweet silhouette waiting at my mother's full on open glass door. She was standing excitedly in the doorway at mom's house when I pulled up. The bright glare of my SUV lights served as the perfect welcoming clue that she had been waiting for. I could see her tiny silhouette in the doorway jumping up and down. She joyfully pointed towards the cobblestone driveway. It was always customary that I would flash my lights three times upon my arrival. This was our game of Morse code. It stood for I love you. When I flashed those three "words" with my SUV lights, she would form her tiny hands and fingers into the shape of a heart and mouth the words "I love you, too! Her nickname was beautiful bright eyes. Her Aunt started calling her this nickname one day. This is because those big beautiful eyes would light up an entire room. As she lay there sleeping, I could not help but notice that her beautiful inner spirit caused an aura to be present upon her. She was truly an earth angel.

Ellie's room was a sight to behold. She was our one and only child. Therefore, her father crowned her as a Princess right there on the examination table during the growth & anatomy ultrasound appointment. He was so very excited. I remember when my husband found out that we were pregnant with a girl, he spared no expense when it came to preparation for Ellie's arrival. He immediately hired the best interior decorator that money could buy. The entire atmosphere was filled with colourful toys and games that would grow with her. She had built-in white book shelves that housed an endless collection of dolls of all colors and sizes. Together, we designed a picture-perfect nursery that would also serve as her "big girl bedroom" once she became older. My husband worked tirelessly to hang custom crown moulding to match ceiling to floor pink sheer curtains that billowed beautifully from a custom-made canopy that hung softly over her convertible crib which was situated in the corner of her room. They were so beautifully paired with cascading handcrafted papier-mache' pink flowers. Ellie was older, so one of the last things that my husband completed for his precious Ellie was to convert her crib turned toddler bed into a full-size bed. He was so very proud of how big his precious princess had become.

As, I placed Ellie in her light blue nightgown and matching head scar, she opened her eyes and gazed into mine. She gave the sweetest smile. I kissed her on the cheek and told her to go and brush her teeth and wash her face. As always, she smiled and said, "Yes mommy." We whispered our customary night time prayer together. We always ended the bedtime prayer by saying, "God did not give me a spirit of fear." This was what was instilled into her after the passing of her father. She regularly expressed fear of darkness and shadows. After a season of nightly prayer and spending time together before bed, Ellie eventually felt comfortable in her own room. I always anointed the house and covered the area with prayer; just as my husband and I did when he was living.

One of my most favorite things about Ellie's room was the beautiful bay window and comfortable, built-in sitting area. Underneath the sitting area were built-in storage containers. Inside there was an endless supply of children's books, bible stories and more. However, there was one book that was especially important to Ellie. This beloved book was the classic children's story "Goodnight Moon", by none other than Margaret Wise Brown. This book allowed us to focus on the simple tasks of getting ready for bed and saying goodnight. Storytime was such an enjoyable time for us. Sometimes, we would sit "criss-cross apple sauce" on Ellie's area rug in what I referred to as her reading nook. Ellie simply called it her book fort. It was a little glam-tent with two plush pillows inside. It was well lit by a few strings of fairy lights that lay gently upon the top of this tiny person's reading hut. It was simple, comfortable and she loved it. I loved it, too.

Next to Ellie's book fort was a table that contained her inhaler, a humidifier and a third epi-pen. I kept one in my purse and one with Ellie's school nurse. She was born slightly premature and her lungs had not fully developed. I received Surfactant injections to aid with her viability. She was starting to need her inhaler less and less. We were so very thankful for this. We lived in a smoke free environment and regularly kept the carpets cleaned to prevent dust and allergens from triggering asthma attacks. Ellie was extremely allergic to strawberries. We were always very careful to steer clear of them. We only had to use her epi-pen once in recent months. We were extremely thankful for this. Overall, Ellie was a happy, healthy little lady. I was so blessed to be called as her mother.

As I kissed her goodnight one last time and tucked her into the bed, I was overcome with emotion. This beautiful child was the tangible evidence of God's hand of mercy in my life. I once thought that I would never be able to bear children. However, God blessed my husband and I to birth this beautiful creature. Her tiny, five-year old hands and feet were a beautiful reminder of God's goodness in our lives. There were so many times that I wished her father was here to share in these snapshots of her life. I turned out her overhead light. I switched on her *Lilo and Stitch* nightlight and gave her one last sweet goodnight kiss.

I walked into my bedroom which was next door to Ellie's room. I had just moved out of our spare bedroom upstairs and back into our marital bedroom because the memories that my husband and I shared were much too great. I was learning to live in the moment. But I struggled with *truly* living and not just existing since my husband's sudden, unexpected departure. On the outside I appeared to have it all together. From my regularly coiffed hair, manicured nails and pedicured feet - to my weekly facials and full body massages; I was taking care of myself, but I still felt lonely and incomplete. I spent enormous amounts of money on products for relaxation and pampering. From body scrubs, candles, perfume and more. Yet, I longed for the touch of someone to love me once more. I longed to lay in my husband's arms one more time.

I missed the beautiful consecration of our union as we made sweet, passionate love. Our mutual saying to one another when we wanted to share our love was "The marriage bed is undefiled!" We would embrace one another tightly. I would lay my head on his chest. He would kiss the top of my head and then we would proceed to undress one another. We enjoyed removing each article of clothing leading up to the moment that we began making sweet, passionate love to one another. Our love possessed a gentleness knitted and intertwined with strength. We shared so many goals and aspirations. The realization as to the totality and sacredness of our love was the welcome climax of our love making. I felt safe with him. He covered me physically and spiritually. He was my protector, provider and priest. Without question our souls were one. I love him still and always will.

We were known as a couple who did not mind public displays of affection, such as holding hands, gentle touches and kisses for no specific reason except to say I love you. We wasted no opportunity to show one another our love and appreciation for what God had given us. We were truly one.

I went into my bedroom and made my way into my bathroom to draw my bath. I gazed up into the skylight above. I could see the starry night that boasted thousands of stars. I usually pretended that the brightest one was my husband saying goodnight to me. As the water continued to run, I sat down at my vanity to remove my make-up. The vanity was filled with makeup brushes every size and color imaginable, blush sets, eye palette collections and a sea of different foundations, concealers and color correcting products. I took a moment to look at myself carefully. I felt like I was a complete mess. People often told me that I was a beautiful woman. But they didn't see the dark circles that took up residence under my well-lined eyes like two dark brown crescent moons. No one knew the amount of concealer it took to mask those nagging dark circles that served as a constant reminder of my lonely situation. As I took out my paddle brush and set of large silver hair clips to wrap my hair, I caught a glimpse of my left hand in the mirror. I still had not gathered the courage to permanently put away my wedding rings. A great deal of time had passed but my heart was still intertwined in the love that my husband and

I had shared. No matter what I accomplished at work, I was still not satisfied. It did not matter what exciting new promotion I obtained, I was still empty. Even when an announcement of a nomination for another service award was presented, I felt hopeless. I was growing tired of sharing my good news with these lonely walls.

As I stepped into my bath, I poured a handful of lavender bath salts into the water. The bubble jets caused them to slowly crack and disperse a sweet smelling and even relaxing fragrance throughout the bathroom. I lit a candle and watched as the flame flickered to and fro. My heart was truly aching. I wiped the silent tears mixed with remnants of foundation and mascara from my face. I stepped into the water and immediately the warmth felt lovely to my tired and aching body.

Once my bath was completed. I went into my walk-in closet to find a pair of pajamas. My walk-in in closet was like my own personal boutique. It was like a place of serenity to me. I had a beautiful black chaise lounge that I loved to sit on and relax. My love for heels was apparent by the vast assortment of colors and styles that decorated the built-in shoe shelving. There was a beautiful spiral chandelier hanging as the focal centrepiece that was situated directly above a shiny black countertop. It sat upon a bright pink rug in the middle of the floor. The wallpaper was black and white striped with gold framed circular mirrors hanging about.

The shiny, black countertop contained my various handbags, sunglasses and accessories. In a golden wire basket, I kept the newest copy of a seasonal nightly devotional book written by a dear friend of mine who is a local author with **_Glory After the Rain Publishing House_**. On this particular night, the passage began with a reading from Psalms which read as follows:

"Psalms 6:6 - I am exhausted as I groan; all night long I drench my bed in tears; my tears saturate the cushion beneath me.

saturate
1: to satisfy fully: satiate.
2: to treat, furnish, or charge with something to the point where no more can be absorbed, dissolved, or retained water saturated with salt.
4: to cause to combine until there is no further tendency to combine.

Tonight, I speak restoration and peace into your various homes. What is it that causes you to lose sleep? What is it that keeps you from experiencing the pre-

determined peace of God? In this hour it is time to no longer allow our pillows to be saturated with this liquid worry called FEAR.

Fear = Faith Erased And Replaced with (Fill in the Blank).

What fear is choking out your faith? What has replaced your faith in this season? It is time to replace anything that is counteracting your faith in God! Let's flip the script and saturate our environments with prayer and praise, instead of tears and fearful tendencies! I speak peace and a saturation of the Holy Spirit to be placed upon you like a spiritual security blanket. We bind bedtime anxiety and panic attacks in the midnight hour. Give us a tangible peace concerning the day ahead. No need to stay awake and worry. Rest well.

Remember: God never sleeps nor slumbers. He is staying awake so that you don't have to."

The accuracy to this devotional journal entry was truly astounding. I quickly realized that I *was* exhausted. Period. I had come to realize that my bed was quickly becoming a slowly sinking lifeboat filled with evidence of recurrent nocturnal tears and unnecessary daytime naps when I was at home alone. My husband's side of the bed was now resting lower than my side because I would find myself lying on his side of the bed more and more as time passed. I often imagined that he was lying there with me. Tears flowed like slow moving liquid testimonials to the pain that I was feeling each moment.

Why did my husband have to leave this world so soon? I did not want to live on without him. I remember asking God why this was my portion. I tried to do what the devotional passage said and saturate my atmosphere with prayer. However, my heart felt as if it were failing me. I found it quite hard to even breath at this point. I was in need of a peaceful rest at this point. However, I could not stop the tears from flowing. As I placed my phone on the charger for the night, I pulled back my bed covers and ascended directly into my bed. As my head touched my down feather pillow, it was as if I was reuniting with a familiar friend. I had become so accustomed to crying into this pillow that it was almost a part of my nightly routine. These tears were not at all forced. There was no one to witness these tears. I never let Ellie see me cry. My friends and family did not truly realize how traumatized I had become. I embraced the realization that depression was, in fact, real. The tremendous number of tears that I released that night were synonymous with the true condition of my heart. I had grown weary of life without my better half. I longed for companionship and love again. I spoke these words out loud into the atmosphere.

Moments later, an unfamiliar number flashed across screen. It was extremely late at night and I had no clue who it could possibly be at this hour. I wondered if it were some sort of emergency about a family member or perhaps a call from my job since I was on call that weekend. I let it ring and ring. It went to voicemail. Shortly thereafter, I received a text. Since I had taken out my contacts, I opened my bedside table's top drawer and pulled out my glasses. I entered my password and swiped my screen. I could not believe what I was reading. To my surprise, the message said:

"Hey beautiful. I haven't been able to stop thinking about you since you pulled out of the shopping mall parking lot. I just wanted to make sure that you made it home ok. I am so sorry for my arrogance a bit earlier when we met. I am not very good at expressing myself. I was hurt as a young child, so I sometimes come across the wrong way. Listen, I know it's late, but I wanted to make sure that you were ok. I can't seem to get you off of my mind. If it's ok, I would really love to talk to you soon…or may I call you now?" The auto signature was listed at the end of the message as *"Broderick P. Morrison III."*

So, his name was Broderick P. Morrison III. I had not even taken a second thought to look at his business card to even see what his name was when we exchanged numbers. To be quite honest, I was not expecting to ever hear from him again. My heart melted when I read that he was often misunderstood as a child.

I thought to myself, "I can't sleep anyways. What would it hurt to speak with him for a few moments?" Besides, he did save the day when he returned my Rover keys. I sat up in bed and pondered the thought of answering him back. If I texted too soon, I might appear desperate. If I waited to long to respond, he might think that I am stuck up or bougie. What would Jesus tell me to do? In my heart, I know that he would tell me that "He maketh me to lie down in green pastures." So maybe I needed to pull back the chartreuse bed covers and take myself on to sleep! But I also felt like I needed a friend at that moment. It would just be harmless conversation, right? My beloved grandmother always said that if you want a good friend, then show yourself friendly. Well, here goes nothing. I said the following words, "Dear wounded self, I pray that you won't regret this later.

I reluctantly texted back to tell him that it was ok to call. I sent a text message that read, "Sure. Call me." Several minutes had passed since my return text. My notifications verified that he saw my message. Yet, he still had not called. I cringed as several more minutes passed before I decided to go ahead and count my losses and go to bed. It was another hour before he called my phone. I was wide awake and staring at the phone with a dismissive attitude as it continued to ring. But I let it roll over to voicemail. He called two more times. I ignored his summons twice more. I guess he finally got the message, because my phone became silent the remainder of the night. I rolled over into my husband's place in our bed. I prayed that the Lord would dry my tears swiftly. Alas, this was not my portion. Liquid grief flowed down my face and onto my already tear stained pillow until midnight turned to morning.

Chapter 5
Words Hurt

My entire life changed on last night. Though I did not fully realize it at the time, life as I knew it would be no more. My beautiful, loving household that was always filled with love and laughter would soon become an unrecognizable den of iniquity. My current status at my job would change and it certainly would not be changing in my favor. There were three simple words that would derail the many plans and long-term goals that I once worked on tirelessly to ascend the invisible career ladder. My stable, promising financial status was about to be turned upside down. Why? It was all because of three simple words. I am not sure if the feelings of melancholy and self-pity were at war with my flesh and gave my mouth an ultimatum that left me no choice but to spew out this untimely reply.

I was usually a very rational being. I purposely took ample opportunity to think things through. I usually err on the side of caution. But for some strange reason my mouth wrote a check that my heart would not be able to cash. I learned that we are most vulnerable when our closest association with our current set of thoughts is an irrational fear, accompanied by endless tears on different days about the same situation. Tears will cloud your natural eyes but also drown out emotional sight and reasoning. My emotional state at the time caused me to toss caution and logical rationales to the wind. I have but myself to blame. After all, I was responsible for selecting and reciting those ten little letters and forming them into a cryptic message which contained only three simple words. It was through these simple yet powerful words that a pandora's box of hurt, loss and betrayal opened with great ease. The key to the chaotic box in question was a sentence that contained the words, "Sure. Call me."

A **word** can be described as single distinct meaningful element of speech or writing, used with others (or sometimes alone) to form a sentence and is typically shown with a space on either side when written or printed. When the element of speech called a **word** is used as a verb, it denotes the act of choosing particular words in order to write or say something. According to Merriam-Webster dictionary, there are an estimated one million words included in the English language to date. Words can be thought of as the smallest unit of speech that can stand by themselves and still have complete meaning. I am fascinated that words create definitions, but that also the use of certain words will *define* the trajectory of your life; sometimes for the rest of your life. Out of the millions of words that I could have selected as my response, why did I choose these three?

Looking back on the situation. I realized that I was extremely vulnerable. I should have taken the necessary steps to keep my emotions reigned in. It had been so long since I had received any attention or validation from a man since the passing of my husband that I spent most of my time working on multiple career projects simultaneously to keep my loneliness at bay. Don't get me wrong. I loved to work and learn, as well as take care of my sweet Ellie. But there was something missing in my life. I secretly desired the companionship and even the loving touch of a man again. I allowed my mouth to speak aloud what my heart was feeling.

As I sat in my room, I contemplated calling him back instead of dealing with the painful agony of waiting for his return call. After all, we are living in a new age where it is perfectly acceptable according to the world's standards to call a man, right? I know this wasn't the way that I was raised, and I feel a sense of desperation concerning this entire matter. Why was I so intrigued by this man's mystery? I saw his arrogance and pride as he leaned upon my car, yet I was willing to overlook the signs of his puffed up and haute spirit…just so that I could fill my own selfish desires. Now, don't get me wrong. As you may have guessed by the title, this man means me no good from start to finish. I am not saying that your story is the same. But I want you to look at my story and see if you may be able to pinpoint some mirrored similarities.

Before I tell you how this story ended up playing out into what you read in the opening chapter, I want to take a few moments to give you some advice on recognizing the signs that lead up to the notorious day. Please read the following pages in this chapter until you see the glory dove on page 34. Once you have completed reading this narrative on bad boys, you will be able to readily pinpoint where I went wrong in my own story. An extremely important fact to remember: watch what a potential partner *says* and compare it with what they *do*. The initial interaction with this man was just what my spirit needed for an awakening. He possessed an air of mystery. He had this whole masculine image and knew all of the right things to say; even though he didn't know me! Because of my own fleshly desires, I had no problem with trusting him. I convinced myself that we would have never seen one another again. Therefore, my behavior would have been "perfectly acceptable". As you will soon find out, quite the opposite is true! The enemy called satan knows exactly the type of desires that resonate with your soul. He will dress it up, cause it to look good, smell great and say all the write phrases that will prompt you to let your guard down. Looking back at the situation. I believe that he was what I would consider…a bad boy.

We all know one. We have all met them. You may have even shared time and space with one. They seem to possess the gift of words and phrases that are used to stroke the deepest recesses of our hearts like finely tuned strings on a precious violin. When they walk into a crowded room, their body subliminally radiates the instrumental version of Fantasia's bad boy anthem **Hood Boys**. My initial interaction with this man was oozing with red flags. The funny thing is that I was so intrigued by his presence, that I didn't even stop to get his name nor ask any questions about his personal life. Yet, this man was holding the keys to my car, leaning on it like he paid the note and did not even introduce himself. He was so confident that I would call him or either accept his call once we exchanged business cards that he didn't give it a second thought. This was not confidence. It was arrogance. I have searched high and low for the answer to a lingering question. Why do good girls like bad boys? The concept of good girls and their strong attraction to bad boys has been around forever. If we look closely in popular books, various types of movies and pop culture, we will easily see instances of good girls meeting up with bad boys and QUICKLY falling head over heels in love. Many times, we truly believe that our love will change these bad boys into better men.

Some women, many of whom consider themselves independent, will say that this is an unrealistic outlook on life. Yet, these are the very same women who will pick up a steamy romance novel with this exact same plot and be emotionally intrigued, biting their lips and wiping sweat from the brow with every turn of the page because of the scene that they have just read. Those of us who are honest will readily admit that while it may seem illogical and our rational side warns us against them, bad boys are highly appealing. The concept of bad boys is a popular theme for a reason: women are attracted to it.

Some people think that what all bad boys have going for them is that they are physically attractive, but I don't think that is the case. Sure, "Prince Charming" was as fine as wine and cool as a summer breeze. But all these bad boys, aka "Prince Charming" are a beautiful sight to behold. Many aren't conventionally physically attractive, but they will still make all the ladies around them swoon and curl their toes. Words and actions are a key factor in the successful capture of prey. Let's take a few moments to see what qualities these bad boys seem to universally possess:

Bad Boys Tend to be Aggressive

I didn't thoroughly question why this man was so comfortable holding on to the keys to my car. Nor, did I explore the reasons that Boutique Associate felt inclined to hand over the keys to my luxury vehicle without much pushback. When I went back to question the associate once this whirlwind was over, I was told that the story that he gave was quite convincing. They also stated that he was very persistent with making sure that I received those keys. There are several reasons why women are drawn to these types of men, but the most overlooked reason, in my opinion, is that they display strong masculine characteristics like aggression. Women want someone who they are confident would knock another man's grill (teeth) out if he looks at her the wrong way, not someone who will cower in fear at conflict. They crave men who are willing to be rough and rowdy to show they care.

Bad Boys Are Usually Very Protective…Even Over Protective

Bad Boys will continue to pursue you until they feel confident that you have taken the bait. They are notorious for acting as if they don't see you close by or will even act as if they are too cool and laid back to care. But if someone or something comes along that threatens you, they'll be the first one to put themselves between you and the threat, physically or emotionally. No matter how tough and strong they appear to be, bad boys usually hate to see women cry. This is especially true if it is their wife or significant other. What makes their protective nature so attractive to some women is that it is usually off guard and totally unexpected. Bad boys are extremely mysterious, and these brief moments serve as a sneak peek into who we truly want to believe this mysterious man is. This is exactly how some men get what they want from an unsuspecting woman. Women view this protective nature as a form of intimacy.

Bad Boys Are Dominant

Dominance and assertiveness are traits that many women find attractive, but few men are willing to display for fear of being considered "too much". Society has made it very hard to display masculine characteristics like this without being perceived as unintelligent, insensitive or barbaric. Men who call the shots inside and outside of the bedroom exude a sense of power, which makes women feel comfortable in being feminine.

Bad Boys Make You Feel A Whole Spectrum of Emotions

This is one of the most profound differences between "good guys" and bad boys. Good guys are consistent and safe. Bad boys tend to be unstable, wild and very unpredictable. Good guys can definitely make you feel good, but bad boys will make you feel ***everything***, even if you resolved that you do not want to. A relationship with a bad boy is often unstable, which is ironically part of their appeal. Women are challenged by this to be someone who the bad boy wants in order to **_keep_** him, so things never get monotonous or boring. Good girls would rather be kept on their toes by mystery and extreme excitement rather than a man who, may appear to be emasculated. Sometimes we as women want to feel a strong rush of different emotions. This is exactly what we are offered through the eloquent words of a bad boy.

Bad Boys Act Confident Bad boys act confident, and confidence is an attractive trait. Unfortunately, their confidence is usually contrived. There are many societal pressures to walk in the spirit of good guy, but there is also a lot of pressure on men to be tough guys or kinder gentler versions of bad boys, if you will! Their strong sense of masculinity gives women the green light to be feminine.

And, another day passed without hearing from my Prince Charming. I looked at his business card once more and decided, that I would just continue to wait for him to call. It had been three whole days since our very first encounter. I was starting to wonder if there was something wrong with me. Had I said something wrong? Had I done something stupid? What was wrong with me? Why hadn't he called? At this point, I am not sure that I am ready for even a friendship with someone of the opposite sex. My life was good at this point, so why mess it up now? I continued to pour myself into my work and the familiarity of the life that Ellie and I were accustomed to. Besides, maybe introducing someone else into Ellie's life was not the best idea at this point in time. I decided that I would just journal my thoughts and desires.

We were approaching the seven-day mark since we last met. I knew that he probably was not interested, so I just began to imagine what I desired from the man that God would send me. After all, I was a strong independent woman. I knew how to live and allow God to sustain me. I was lonely, often bitterly bereaving and just plain lost. I needed an intervention. I decided to start writing. Here is one of the journal entries that I made:

Dear Lord. It has been so very long since I have been in the arms of my dear husband. I miss him dearly. I miss the way that he made me feel so safe. I miss the way that he prayed over our household and business dealings. I truly desire to feel loved, wanted and safe again. God, I am still young. My heart longs to be with someone. God my spirit is so willing, but my flesh is very weak.

Why have you forgotten me Lord? I feel uncovered. I feel as if you no longer care about me. I wish that the hands of time could stand still once more, so that I could be with my husband again. But you took him from me without warning or even the ability to say goodbye. I am lost and angry. I need love.

-   *Signed Lady with the Broken Heart*

The acknowledgement in the heavenly realm that included this sequence of words in my journal coupled with an additional three words that I had previously uttered (sure call me), were a recipe for disaster in the spirit realm. The saying goes that we should hush until we are healed. The enemy (called satan) knows the true condition of our hearts and he is fully aware of our desires. By the same token, he is also fully aware of who it is that he can use to get our undivided attention. I placed my heart on my sleeve. I moved about in an unfamiliar way over those next few days. I expressed under an open heaven my true heart's desire. The problem with that is the fact that the enemy was also listening. I was out of character.

After I completed journaling on that seventh day, I prepared to wrap my hair and get ready for bed. I looked forward to taking a long hot bath and sliding into my silky sheets. I was especially lonely on this day, because my sweet Ellie was spending the next two weeks with her grandparents. The house was lonely. I was lonely. And, because I missed my husband…my bed was lonely. It had been so hard to move my thinking from married to single. And it was not helpful that most people viewed singleness as a curse or some incurable disease. The world seemed to be tailored to couples. I was still trying to find my way as a woman without a covering. I still went to church and read God's word. I didn't realize it at the time, but my relationship with God was severely strained because I still blamed him for my loss. I blamed him for Ellie's loss of a father figure. Truth be told…I was angry. I began to lash out at God and the tears began to fall. I was tired. I wanted to love and be loved again. Looking back, I realized that my focus was all wrong. When you rearrange your priorities without counting up the cost, you are in grave danger of going emotionally, physically and spiritually bankrupt!

In an act of pure desperation, I picked up my cell phone and stared at the business card that had been placed on my night stand for seven whole days. I took a deep breath in and dialled the first few digits. I took another deep breath and dialled the last number. I waited for that silky-smooth voice to pick up on the other end. On the fourth ring, I started to hang up. But suddenly I heard the words "Hey baby girl." My heart melted. I lost my breath when he answered the phone. I am most certain that he could both see and hear my giddy smile through the phone. He asked me how I had been and anchored the end of the question with the word "beautiful". I felt so honored that he would even consider asking me this question during such a hard time. He explained that he had been meaning to call but he was intimidated by my "extraordinary beauty". He also mentioned that he would love to have some time alone…away from my friends. He wanted to "get to know me better." The fact that he saw beauty in me made me feel more valuable. I was astonished at the great many things that we had in common. He mentioned some of the same places that I had travelled, we loved the same restaurants and even used the same mechanic for our similar vehicles. I felt that this man *truly* wanted to get to know me better and after talking on the phone until the sun came up the next morning, I was ready to let him.

Let's pause for a moment. What was the deciding factor for continuing this pursuit you ask? Words. Nothing more. Nothing less. Just words. Words that would be the blueprint for the recalculation of life as I knew it. Later, I would learn that these words were empty phrases that sounded very convincing when used in a certain sequence mixed with the right amount of seemingly genuine emotion.

Over a very short time frame, these seemingly genuine words would transcend from loving and kind to a repeatedly harsh use of hurtful words and phrases. There would be deeply cutting four letter words. On several occasions, this man became quite comfortable using a five-letter word that no self -respecting woman wishes to be associated with. Time would pass and the use of the word meaning female dog became more and more common within our "relationship". The reason according to Prince Charming was the fact that he was "afraid of losing me…." or something out of my control would happen and my mouth would form itself to express a one-word complete sentence that simply said "no."

This man would soon grow comfortable using this five-letter word as a **verb, or action word** to describe what he felt I was doing when I expressed dissatisfaction at a bright idea that he possessed did not seem like a mature nor reasonable request. According to "Prince Charming", I was b****ing.

He also used this word as a **noun - a person, place or thing** to express his disapproval at my clothes, nails or hair. According to him, I was walking around looking like a "whore like b****h." In the end, the very thing that he said originally drew me to him, worked as a thorn in his side. It caused me to be confused about my self-worth because I was at a fragile state where my self esteem and personal worth were contingent upon how *he* felt about me. Instead of the words she when referring to me on the phone with his homeboys, this five-letter word became a **pronoun – which is used to replace a noun.** I was no longer she or her. He confidently referred to me as "my b****".

Over time, "Prince Charming" easily used this five-letter word as an **adjective or describing word**. The use of this five- letter word went from a contested argument to easily becoming a one-word sentence. Please believe me when I tell you that words truly hurt. They cut down deep into the soul. Their wounds are able to penetrate even the strongest of us. The effects are brutal and long lasting. The funny thing is that there is a space or a pause on either side of a word when it is in written form. There is no such space nor pause once those words leave your tongue. Again, I say to you; words hurt.

Chapter 6
*G*uard Your Heart

Last night, we talked on the phone until midnight turned into the early morning. I can still feel the obliterated light shine through the blinds and onto to my back as I turned over to realize that my phone was on 3% battery life. I was so excited to have some male conversation again that I neglected to cut the call short, so that I could place my phone on the wireless charger. One of the first questions that I asked Prince Charming was the reason why he had acted so very arrogant at our initial meeting. He softly laughed and explained that he felt intimidated by my beauty and apparent success, as evidenced by my carefree, modern physical appearance, choice of sisterhood and means of transportation. He wanted to show me that he was confident. Instead, he came across as pompous and arrogant. He said, this was the reason that he failed to call. However, he did say that he had a feeling that I would definitely call him. He said that he waited patiently, just praying that I would "find him worthy".

Wow, he wanted *me*? He was waiting for me to show *him* that he was worth talking to? With this notion, I thought that God was sending me a kind-hearted man who could relate to having issues with acceptance. Maybe I could understand him and sympathize with him. As we talked about life in general, we soon discovered that we shared the same story. As it turns out, he had lost his wife during childbirth to one of their five children...yes five children. Three of the five were in High School and the oldest two were in college. They seemed to be extremely close in age. I listened intently as he explained how his wife had died during the birth of their youngest son. He cried and became silent at some points. Although I did not know this man fully, I listened. After all, my story was quite similar. Except I had not died in child birth. Our youngest daughter did. And, I had lost my spouse in a motorcycle accident. We dried our tears and continued to talk about numerous things throughout the night. Suddenly, I did not feel lonely any longer. I felt understood.

I was so fascinated by all of the amazing things that we were mutually interested in. I loved art. He loved art. I loved to travel. He loved to travel. When I asked him about his favorite place to visit, he never gave a clear answer. When I asked him why, he said "I can show you better than I can tell you." As it turns out he has visited over 12 countries. Wow! He seemed to be a globe trotter. We talked about Santorini Greece, which was on my bucket list with my homegirls for the following year. When I asked had he been there, he said that he had been twice already. When I inquired about great excursions for four single ladies traveling alone, he became quiet. I looked at my phone to see if he was still on the line. It appeared that the line had died during the last part of the conversation. I could not believe that we were on the phone for 8 hours straight. I smiled and looked forward to our next encounter.

I enjoyed our conversation on last evening, and smooth on into this morning. But truth be told, a sister was tired! This particular weekend was an alternate weekend for hair and nails. Ellie was staying at her grandparents and so I decided that I would sleep in since I had spent so many hours on the phone with Prince Charming. I also figured that I should start calling him by his government name since we were getting to know one another.

Broderick P. Morrison III. His name sounded sturdy. It was a good name. It sounded like a name that carried weight. It was professional sounding and rolled off the tongue with ease. The "III" at the end of his name was interesting. I wondered what fascinating family lineage was attached to those three letters. What was his father like? Or, even his grandfather? What was the secret behind this mystery man? We had talked for what seemed like an eternity. And the abrupt disconnection only intensified my desire to learn more. He seemed to know all the right things to say. It appeared that he knew me much more than I knew him. How could he know just what to ask? How did we like all of the same things? At this point, I am not too concerned with the reason why. I was excited about our conversation. I know it is not a relationship or anything right now, but I was thankful for the interaction. Hmm…this is news worthy. I guess I will go ahead and update my Facebook status. While I am at it, I may as well let my followers on Instagram and Twitter know as well. It's just harmless fun…right?

So, my social media update went something like this: *"That moment when you are out with your homegirls and you meet the real life equivalent of Prince Charming. Smooth brown skin, award winning smile and smells so very good. Let's just say, we talked on the phone until yesterday turned into today. #Melanin #HeIsSoFine #BeStillMyHeart"*

I sent this update to all three accounts. Prior to my husband's death, we had a shared account and neither of us posted very much. Well since I was now single and traveling with my girlfriends all the time, I figured I would live and enjoy life. I posted Ellie and I at the hair salon, nail salon and favorite shopping mall. I also posted about all of my upcoming trips and even our favorite restaurants. I loved posting pictures and that is exactly what I did. I loved updating my status. It was almost like a way to prove to myself that I was still living and not just existing. I seemed to have fallen into a selfish season as my usual routine had gotten off course.

It wasn't long until Broderick called back and said that he wanted to spend some "quality time" with me this weekend. I told him that I was available and asked him what time I should expect him to pick me up. To my surprise, he asked that I meet him at the same place where we first met. I was a little confused as to the reason why, but I didn't question it (big mistake).

As requested, I headed to the local mall to meet up with Broderick. I stood patiently by the escalator in the local mall where we first met. I was a bit early. So, naturally I just took a few minutes to update my Facebook status so that my homegirls could see my whereabouts. Besides…no one else would possibly be following my status, right? My hair was looking extra silky that day, so I snapped an Instagram photo, too. About 20 minutes had passed and suddenly, I started to turn around when I felt the presence of someone behind me. Before I could spin my body all the way around, his big strong arms caught me in mid twirl. My long silky curls covered my shoulders and upper back. He leaned over and moved my hair gently off my face. He kissed me softly on the cheek from behind Then, he proceeded to kiss me on the forehead. My Lord, this felt so good! I remember, when my husband used to do this to me. As a matter of fact, I recall a picture of this very pose on my Instagram page. The smell of Davidoff Cool Water cologne was once again captivating my nostrils. Only this time I was very aware of his physical presence. As we walked away towards the food court, he gently looked into my eyes and placed his hand onto mine. I dropped my head like a school girl. My soft curls moved just right as I lifted my head and smiled.

We decided to have lunch in the food court. I was on a health kick, and so was he it seemed. We both ordered veggie burgers and sweet potato fries. I loved cucumber water. But, as it turns out, he was allergic to cucumbers. I thought it was quite strange that he ordered a veggie burger. But once again I didn't question it. I was thoroughly enjoying our conversation. Afternoon turned to evening as we walked throughout the mall hand in hand. Suddenly, he whipped out is phone to take a selfie. He kissed me on the cheek and snapped away. Then, I noticed that he turned his phone off. Our eyes locked and I asked why he didn't leave it on in case his children called. He stated that they were away with their grandmother this weekend. He said that once I agreed to spend time with him today, he made arrangement for us to spend quality time together…the entire weekend…alone. We talked hours upon hours about our individual life goals and ambitions.

One thing leads to another and afternoon became dusk. We headed to the parking lot and decided to sit in my car and talk. He said that his car was parked on the opposite side of the mall, so sitting in my car made perfect sense. It was mutually decided that we would go back to my condominium to watch movies and relax. It feels as if this man has cast a spell upon me. He is supplying me with everything that my heart desires. I feel safe with him. I don't ask many questions for fear of running him away. I felt obligated to just enjoy the moment. I missed my dear husband so desperately. I wanted to live in the moment, and I did just that.

Deborah Cox once sang a hit song titled "How did you get here? Nobody is supposed to be here!" This is the part of the story where I threw caution to the wind. For the first time in a very long time, I fully let my guard down. I also let my hair down, as well as my bra straps and matching panties. Modesty was scattered across the floor. Why was I doing this? I had always taken pride in doing the right thing. A tear ran down my face as I began to feel remorse, fear, regret and uncertainty all at the same time. I noticed that he alternated between being a bit too rough and then catching himself and becoming extremely tender. It had been a tremendous amount of time since I had been made love to. I wouldn't exactly call this love. We had only just met. My husband was my College sweetheart. He was my first. He was the only man that I had ever known. I kept saying that I wasn't sure if I was ready for such a big step. He reassured me and told me to relax. He repeatedly kissed me softly on the cheek and forehead. Maybe it would be okay just this one time…

I had started out calling him "Prince Charming". But, by the end of the night, this changed. I was calling him by his government given name. The level of ecstasy that he made my body feel on that infamous night left no question. The neighbors *definitely* knew his name.

Why had I acted as if I didn't know what the word of God said. I had made a promise to myself that I would wait until God sent me the right one if I were ever to marry again. Why did I allow him to see my naked body in all of its glory? My husband's picture was still sitting on my nightstand in the silver picture frame that we purchased while in Niagara Falls. I looked over and noticed that Broderick had placed it face down. I felt ashamed.

After it was over, I laid there on my side of the bed facing the wall. I felt a range of emotions as I looked over my shoulder at this man who now occupied my husband's space in our marital bed. I asked myself again, how in the world I ended up here. I was an extremely bright, successful young woman and I just did not understand what was happening to me. As I completed an analysis of the situation at hand, I realized that I had allowed my guard to be let down. I was allowing my emotions to make decisions based on what I was feeling. Feelings are temporary. Decisions like the one that I just made could very well have lasting implications. I could have gotten pregnant. I could have contracted an STD. Even worse, I could have been looked upon differently because of what just took place. I turned over in desperation to talk about what had just taken place. He opened his eyes briefly and asked if we could talk about this in the morning. He kissed me on the cheek. I became quiet. He quietly said in a soft yet masculine tone, "Come here." He held me through the night. I was reassured that everything was going to be ok. I slept well.

The next morning, I woke up feeling quite strange. My spirit was unsettled. I could not believe what had taken place. I was praying that it was all a dream. I had never had this feeling of shame before. My husband and I had waited until marriage for sex. I never felt dirty like this before. I was met with an overwhelming amount of anxiety. I jumped out of bed and realized that I had not even showered nor wrapped my hair last night. I felt unclean and dishevelled.

I felt so out of place in my own home. I glanced over at Broderick as he slept. My feelings were that of confusion and fear. I decided to go into the en suite bathroom and get myself together. At that moment, I quickly realized that I had to teach Sunday School and I had not even taken out the time to prepare the lesson!

I stepped into the shower and just began to let the water wash all the invisible dirt and shame away. Half way through my shower, the body cherry almond body wash was met with a mixture of my tears and the newfound potion made its way down my face and disappeared into the drain. I was certain that the entire Sunday School class would be able to see what I had taken part in last night. I said to myself, "I may as well wear a Scarlet Letter."

As I stepped out of the shower, I walked hurriedly into my closet vanity area. I selected a nice conservative suit for the morning service. Thankfully I had picked up my dry cleaning on Wednesday. My spirit was so uneasy. I suddenly had no desire to even be close to this man. I couldn't trust my emotions. A sense of anger and regret rose up within my spirit. I felt off balance as I pulled my hair into a high ponytail. I hadn't worn my hair in a high pony tail since the day Ellie was born. I had no choice this morning because I did not prepare my hair last night before "going to bed." I placed my dress over my head and onto my body. I laid my jacket across the chaise lounge for the time being. I had made up in my mind that I was going to end these shenanigans with Prince Charming right now. It was fun while it lasted, but it was time to count my losses and get back to normal.

I stepped barefoot onto the hardwood that lead from the closet vanity to my bedroom. I walked towards my California king size bed and to my surprise…it was empty. Where was Broderick? I initially thought that maybe he had gone into the second bathroom or even to the kitchen to grab something to eat. I realized that I hadn't even given him a full tour of the house, so I began to call his name. I called his name several times and did not receive an answer. I went back into the bedroom. I checked to see if he had left a note. Nothing was left in sight.

I thought to myself, "How crass of him! He didn't even leave a note." I felt so used all over again. But I did realize that I had played an equal part in this foolishness. I guess he called an Uber or Lyft as I was showering. He had conveniently left his own car in the parking lot at the mall. Oh well. Breathe in. Breath out. Regroup. That is the plan.

I finished preparing myself for morning worship service and made a quiet resolve that I would not allow this type of situation to cloud my judgement ever again. I was very thankful that Ellie was still at her grandparent's house. I had never had another man in our home since her father passed. As a matter of fact, I had not "had" another man *period* since her father died. I lifted my husband's picture off the night stand and gave it a gentle kiss. I was sure that he was looking back at me through the picture frame glass with a look of disappointment. I whispered to him that I was sorry. I know it seemed silly. But I loved this man so very much. I missed him terribly.

I went into the closet to grab my suit jacket and my purse. I noticed that some items on the vanity counter looked out of place. I noticed that my Bible was lying upside down on the floor. Additionally, my phone was missing. I thought to myself that I must have left it in the car on the charger. I needed to get it together. I reached into my purse to get my keys, but then I remembered that I hung them on a hook close to the foyer entryway when we came in last night. I slid on my Red Bottoms and headed towards the entryway. I caught a glimpse of myself in the large wall mirror on the way to the foyer. I looked horrendous this morning. I felt like the bags under my eyes would be a dead give away as to what ungodly shenanigans had taken place the previous night. I pressed on towards the foyer. When I got to the wall hook where I periodically hung my keys, there was nothing there. I was dumbfounded. Something told me to check the drive way. I reluctantly turned the door knob. I stood in amazement as my front door slowly swung open. My Range Rover was gone!

I could not believe what was happening. In my haste, I ran with mad speed to my bedroom to retrieve my phone. At that moment, I remembered...my phone was in the car! I was panicking hysterically. Why was this happening to me? Why had I been so stupid? What was I thinking? I allowed this man into my home and this is what he has done! I started to go next door to see if I could borrow their phone to call his phone, my phone and/or the police (not necessarily in that order). I got ready to knock on the door, but I stopped myself and just slid my hand down the door. I had acted completely out of character the night before. I was certain that my neighbors on all sides had witnessed this strange man enter my home and not leave until darkness turned to day. I tiptoed back into my house in shame. I pulled out my tablet to contact my homegirls on group chat through Facebook. But I quickly hung up once I realized how pathetic I would sound when I told them what had transpired. I would be missing church today. I sent my Pastor a Facebook message to let him know that I would be unable to attend services this morning. I had never missed a Sunday School service in the 14 years that I had attended the church. He wanted to know if all was well because I had reached out through the church Facebook account instead of just placing a phone call. I lied and said that I was under the weather and didn't have a voice to talk. Truth be told, I did in fact feel quite ill. However, the real truth was stranger than fiction.

I waited for hours for some sign of my vehicle and my cell phone to show up. I suddenly started to feel paranoid and violated. How did he have the courage to do such a thing. It is almost as if he knew that my reaction would be one of unspoken submission and subsequent defeat.

To my surprise there was a note that had fallen under the bed that simply said, "My son is very ill. I didn't know what to do so I grabbed your keys and headed out. I am so sorry it was an emergency." For some strange reason this brought only a slight satisfaction to my spirit. I was still quite angry. I was set to leave for our International girl's trip that coming Thursday morning. I had a special hair appointment scheduled for Monday after work. I felt nervous and off track. But I was determined that once this whole thing was settled with my car and cell phone – it was good bye for Prince Charming. I spent the remainder of the day cleaning, packing and crying. I also washed my bed linens…twice. It was time to reclaim my environment.

Around 11:30 pm, I was sitting downstairs watching a movie, still waiting on Broderick to return when I saw a bright light shine into the driveway. I jumped up and looked through the front door. He was sitting in the car smiling and talking on the phone and all seemed to be well. Another twenty minutes passed before he came to the door. I could hear him on the front porch. But to my great surprise he invited himself right on in. He walked in as if nothing had transpired. He looked at me and said, "Hey baby!" as he carelessly threw my key ring and key fob over onto the entry way table. I was in complete shock! This negro walked into my home without knocking, threw MY car keys carelessly over onto the entry table after technically stealing my car for the day?!?! I must be dreaming. I stood up and asked him what he was thinking!

What he said next, I would have never imagined in a million years. He looked at me and said the following words, *"You don't own me. You can't tell me what to do! You weren't coming with all of that attitude when you were screaming my name last night! I left a f****** note. If you didn't read it, then that's on you! For someone with so much education you sure are stupid!"* I was in complete shock. I had never been spoken to by anyone in this manner. What had I done? I walked towards him and let him know that I would not be spoken to in that manner. I asked him where he had been and why had he left me here with no phone and without a car. At that moment, he broke down crying. He walked towards me and fell to his knees. It is as if he went from one extreme to the next in a matter of moments. I had in fact gotten the note. So, I thought to myself that maybe he was under a great deal of pressure. Maybe he didn't mean it. The motherly nurse trait arrived on the scene. I let him stay at my feet and cry for what seemed like half an hour. Finally, when he settled down, I asked how his son was doing. He said that everything was ok with his son. Then, he asked if I would just hold him. And, I did. I figured that his anger must be due to the stress of the day. I remembered how he listened as I poured my heart out about the loss of my husband. I thought would only be right that I listened to him as well. And so, I did this as well.

Two more hours passed. It was time for me to prepare for the day ahead. I told him that he would need to call a rideshare company because it was late, and I had to prepare for work in the morning. I had a whole routine and I was not feeling too confident about straying away from my routine. I explained that I didn't think that we should sleep together anymore. At first, he said nothing. He just hung his head. Then, he looked at me with those brown eyes and asked if I was going to abandon him "like all the others when I needed them?" We held one another on the couch until midnight became morning.

Important Chapter Reflection** Every move that Ellie and I made was like clockwork. We had a set pattern and a set time to do things. It was not until it was too late that I realized that in fact, this was the very reason that this man was preying on us. Once I gave him my name, all he had to do was follow my posts on Social media. He had all my thoughts and desires at his fingertips. He was able to see that I was widowed. He took an entire week to surf through my pictures of past vacations, my wedding album, etc. He was also able to see that I lived alone and even where I lived because of Social Media. He saw a pic that I tagged when my husband bought the Range Rover. We are standing in our driveway and as it turns out, the intersecting street signs were clearly visible. My heart was broken behind the passing of my husband. I did not recognize how vulnerable I made myself. We had received a sizable life insurance benefit a few months after his burial. I had not spent a penny of it, except to pay off the car and the house. The remainder was placed into a savings account for Ellie. My life was like an open book to this man, as well as the rest of the world.

Take a moment to reflect on your daily habits. Are you unknowingly placing yourself at risk for harm? Are the details of your life too accessible to others? How can someone truly get to know us as a prerequisite to dating or even friendship, if our every move is detailed proudly on Social Media? It is especially important to keep our little ones safe as well. Are you checking the internet for sexual predators? Are there any red flags that send up a danger signal? PLEASE do not ignore the signs. All it takes is one moment of carelessness to potentially change the course of your life. Sometimes there will not be a second chance to repair what was damaged. Lives will be affected and even lost. Ask me how I know.

Be fully aware of your trackability online

How much information can be found out about you online? Have you ever Googled yourself? If not, you should, just so you can be aware of what personal information is out there about you.

Try different combinations. Start with just your full name. Then try your name plus your phone number, your name plus your home address, and your name and your birthdate.

You can also use a Google image search with the same information to see what sites may be hosting information about you. Do not be shy about searching for yourself on social networks, too. You can also search for your family members to see what information is available about you through their profiles.

If you find that your sensitive personal information is easily available, there are a few ways you can get it removed from the internet.

In many cases, if a website has information such as your address, telephone number, date of birth, or photo, you will have to contact the website and ask to have the data removed.

If it's sensitive personal information such as your Social Security number, bank account, or credit card number, you can contact Google and they will remove it.

Report cyberstalking

If you encounter someone that is engaging in cyberstalking behaviors and it seems serious, or you begin to receive threats, you should report it to the police. Keep in mind many police departments have cybercrime units, and cyberstalking is a crime.

If you're being cyberstalked, remember to keep a copy of any message or online image that could serve as proof. Use the "print screen" or other keyboard functions to save screenshots.

If you suspect that someone is using spyware software to track your everyday activities, and you believe you may be in danger, only use public computers or telephones to seek help. Otherwise, your efforts to get help will be known to your cyber stalker and this may leave you in even greater danger.

$\mathscr{I}$NTRODUCING

$\mathscr{E}$llie

$\mathscr{D}$omestic $\mathscr{V}$iolence
As Seen
Through the Eyes of Small Children

written by
Mikayla Thompson

52

Chapter 7
*L*ove Doesn't Hurt

Hello. My name is Elizabeth. But mommy calls me Ellie. Sometimes she even calls me Ellie Pooh! I'm 5 years old. Yep! That many. I like running, skipping, and jumping on each square of the sidewalk! I can't ride a bike just yet because daddy hadn't taken off my training wheels before he went to heaven. But that's a story for another time. Anyways, I like to do lots and lots of fun things with mommy. In the mornings she likes to put my hair in two big puffs. I always tell her to put two different color scrunchies on my hair. I like to wear blue and pink because it reminds me of cotton candy. Then she lets me dress myself up any way that I like! My mommy is so much fun.

I like to put on my best-est princess dresses and go to the mall. We love to get our feet done. I always get excited to see Ms. Lulu! She tickles my feet with the suds and bubbles. She paints my toes and fingernails. I feel like a big girl when I get to go see Ms. Lulu. Mommy and I laugh and have so much fun together all day until we're both *really* hungry. Then, she'll get my favorit-est food.... PIZZA!! I love pizza! Mommy says I am saying it wrong, but I like lots of "cinderella cheese" on my pizza. She calls is moza…mozar…mozzarella, yes that's it. But I think cinderella cheese sounds better. I couldn't forget pineapples and spicy sausage! We like to stuff our faces and then we get to eat sweet treats afterwards! My most favorite ice cream in the whole wide world is the same as daddy's; chocolate chip rocky road with sprinkles. When I get tired from our long day, I usually fall asleep on the way home. Mommy will carry me from the car to my room and put me in my night clothes. But my most favorite part, is when mommy falls asleep in *my* bed during thunderstorms. Cause then I have my mommy **and** my Otie to cuddle. Otie is my teddy bear. He's blue with one button eye, cause one of the buttons are missing. He also has orange stitches that unravel just a little. Mommy said that she would get me a new one, but I told her that I like him just the way he is; button or no button! I love my mommy so much. She's warm and she always smells like hazelnut and mommy hugs! And sometimes when she hugs me, I can feel daddy hugging both of us in spirit. I miss daddy sometimes. I wish I could remember him all the way. I just remember me, him, and mommy walking in the park. I was on his shoulders and laughing with sprinkles and ice cream all over my face. I wish he were still here. After he died, mommy let me keep his college shirt. I put it on my Otie bear! That's why Otie means so much to me. I had him when I was little when daddy was still here. I had him when I saw daddy for the last time in the church. He was laying in front of the church in a long box sleeping. He wouldn't wake up anymore.

My Otie bear has been there with me when I laughed or cried. He even protects me from monsters in the dark. Nothing could replace the love I have for my bear and mommy.

$\mathscr{M}$onsters in The Dark

One day, mommy picked me up from school and she seemed really excited. I looked at her and said, "Why are you so happy mommy?" I asked. I didn't give her time to answer. Mommy answered back and said, "Let's go get some pizza!" I hadn't seen mommy this happy since daddy got her tulips on her birthday. "I want you to meet a friend of mommy's!" she said. We made our way to *Pizzeria Planet* and a man was standing at the door with a purple rose. He was really tall; almost like a basketball player! Mommy smiled and waved at him as soon as she parked the car. She came to the back door to help me out of my booster seat. I reached for her and she picked me up and held me on her hip. We walked towards the tall man. As we came closer, mommy said "Ellie, this is mommy's friend Mr. Broderick. Say hello!" I looked at him and waved. But for some reason I turned away and laid my head on her shoulder.

Normally, mommy and I play arcade games and stuff our faces with pizza. But, this time, all they did was talk and mommy decided to eat salad instead of pizza. I didn't say much the whole time we were there together. Not until mommy went to the bathroom and I was left with Mr. Broderick for a minute when mommy said, "I'll be right back, I'm going to go powder my nose." Then I said, "Mommy what's that mean?" I asked. Instead of mommy answering, Mr. Broderick talked for her. He said, "It means your mother is going to go fix her hair, straighten her necklace and stuff like that." he said. My eyes lit up. Then, I giggled and said "Oh, well why didn't you just say that mama?" Mommy's face turned red as she bent down to kiss me on the cheek.

Mr. Broderick and I sat patiently for the waiter to bring our pizza. He tried to talk to me, but I was a little shy. He didn't say much of anything after that. I felt bad for ignoring him. Mommy always says ignoring is rude. I heard the doors swing open by the kitchen and a familiar voice shouted,

"Ellie Bean!" It was my favorite waiter named Ashton! Ashton has always

been so nice to me and mommy. He always makes sure to take care of us.

Sometimes he sneaks me extra brownies from the kitchen! We even have

a special fist bump. After we did our special fist bump, Ashton said, "Sorry

Ellie Bean, we don't have any spicy sausage today. We had a meat-lovers

special and an entire high school football team came in after their game

and cleaned us out! But I did manage to get you a brownie kiddo!" I smiled

from ear to ear. But before I could say thank you, I looked over and

noticed Mr. Broderick was huffing and puffing like the wolf from that

book my teacher read to us in class. He started yelling at Ashton really

loud. I had to cover my ears and close my eyes. He seemed to be really

upset over our pizza order. He stood up and grabbed Ashton's shirt eally

hard. Ashton looked really scared. I felt bad because I wanted to help

Ashton, but I couldn't move because I was so scared too. Before Mr.

Broderick let him go he said "Instead of coming out here playing around,

pay attention and get my order right next time. Get it RIGHT!" I felt like

a bad friend after watching Ashton run to the kitchen in fear. I couldn't

help my friend. Finally, mommy came out of the bathroom and asked him

what was all the noise that she heard. "Oh, just some high school kid

spazzed on me." Mommy looked very confused and said, "You mean

Ashton? Broderick that doesn't sound anything like him! Let me go talk to him." she said. Mr. Broderick grabbed her wrist before she went to the kitchen. It almost looked like it hurt mommy. He said, "Are you calling me a liar?" Then Mommy looked down at her wrist and the looked back at him and jerked it away. She told Mr. Broderick, "All I am saying is that this is not like Ashton. Cut the kid some slack. I'm sure he probably just got a bad grade on a math test and he's just a little flustered. It's okay. I sometimes tutor Ashton" I tugged on mommys' dress and said, "Mommy I want my Otie Bear." Mommy looked down and asked me what was wrong. I was scared to say anything about what I saw, so I told her that Otie was lonely and I wanted to hug him. I didn't mean to, but I started to cry. "I'd better get her home. Mr. Broderick was trying to get her to stay. Everybody in the Pizzeria was looking at us funny; especially Ashton and the short man that they called a man..mana..manager.

I was so sad because everyone was looking at us funny. I shouted out, "Mommy I want my Otie Bear!" I shouted and screamed and cried. I wanted my Otie Bear. I wanted my mommy and most of all I missed my daddy. He always knew what to do. "I'll call you" he said. Mommy just looked at everyone looking at us. She looked at Ashton with tears in her eyes and whispered, "I'm so sorry." Then, she held my hand until we got to the car and we drove home.

6 months later...

For some reason, mommy keeps having funny spots on her face and arms. It looked like the boo-boos that I get when I fall off my bike or fall down on the ground. I wonder why there are so many of them? Mommy says that she fell down stairs or she bumped into the doorway. Mommy has never been this clumsy. I am worried. I have been practicing learning my colors. Mommy's skin looks blue. Sometimes the marks are black too. Her eye looks funny, so she puts on makeup...but I can still see it.

I miss the old mommy. This is the third time this week that my grandparents have picked me up from kindergarten. Mommy's been really busy with work. Mr. Broderick always drives mommy and daddy's car now. I hope she won't keep being his friend. Mr. Broderick is really scary. He yells at mommy a lot. If he is her friend, why does he hurt her?

I've been spending so much time with my grandparents lately. I love my Granny and Pee-paw, but I don't see much of mommy any more. I worry about her because we used to spend every day together and now, she doesn't have energy to play anymore. Sometimes, my mommy cries.

One night while I was at my grandparent's house, I was supposed to be sleeping, but I wanted to sneak some cookies from Pee-paws cookie bin. I was tiptoeing down the hallway and I heard Granny talking on the phone in the kitchen. I sat down behind the door hiding. It sounded like she was talking to mommy. My granny didn't really sound very happy. She almost started yelling until I poked my head around the corner and said, "Granny is that my mommy?" She looked at me and said, "Ellie, baby, why are you up? I didn't tell her that I was looking for cookies. I asked her if she was talking to mommy and she shook her head like she was saying yes. My eyes lit up. "Yay! I want to talk to mommy!" I kept jumping up and down like a jumping bean. I tried to jump to get the phone and she finally gave it to me. "Hi mommy!" It sounded like mommy was crying, because she sniffed her nose and said, "Ellie bean, I miss you too."

She kept saying over and over that she missed me and loved me so much. Then, finally she told me to get back to bed. missed me and loved me and to get back to bed. I told her that I would. But, before I let go of the phone, I shouted. "Where are you mommy?!" Granny told me that she was with a friend. I didn't want it to be Mr. Broderick

because he was scary. I asked granny if she was with Mr. Broderick.

Granny didn't answer. I told granny to tell my mommy that he had the

cooties and it wasn't safe to be around him! She told me to give Granny

the phone back and I handed it back to her. I heard granny say, "Please.

Just be careful daughter." Then she hung up the phone.

She grabbed my hand and walked me to my room. On the

way, I looked up to her and asked, "Why doesn't mommy

love me anymore? We used to spend so much time together and now

we barely see each other. Have I been bad?" Then, Granny kneeled

down to me and put her hands on my face. "No, sweet little Ellie Pooh,

you weren't bad at all. You are a perfect little angel. Mommy is dealing

with some things right now, but everything will be alright after tonight.

Watch and see! I believed my granny.

Important Chapter Reflection** According to the Office on Women's Health, many children exposed to violence in the home are also victims of physical abuse. Children who witness domestic violence or are victims of abuse themselves are at serious risk for long-term physical and mental health problems. Children who witness violence between parents may also be at greater risk of being violent in their future relationships. If you are a parent who is experiencing abuse, it can be difficult to know how to protect your child.

Each child responds differently to abuse and trauma. Some children are more resilient, and some are more sensitive. How successful a child is at recovering from abuse or trauma depends on several things, including having:

- A good support system or good relationships with trusted adults
- High self-esteem
- Healthy friendships

Although children will probably never forget what they saw or experienced during the abuse, they can learn healthy ways to deal with their emotions and memories as they mature. The sooner a child gets help, the better his or her chances for becoming a mentally and physically healthy adult.

For more information, please go to:
https://www.womenshealth.gov/relationships-and-safety/domestic-violence/effects-domestic-violence-children

*Remember: Be sure to erase your browser window history if you feel that you may be in danger of your abuser discovering your desire for domestic violence assistance.

Glory After the Rain Ministries

CHAPTER 8
Who Is This Woman?

It was so good to hear Ellie's sweet voice. When I hung up the phone with my mother, her last words to me were "Daughter, you are not tired yet. When you really get tired you will do something about it!" My first instinct was to be offended. But as I sat in silence on the other end of the phone line, I realized that she was absolutely right. I was responsible for securing my own happiness. My main focus had moved from taking care of Ellie and I, to walking on egg shells to keep the peace with Broderick. At times it was hard to believe that this was my life. I felt like I was numb to the world. Most times, I was in a daze. I wasn't sure if it was because of the verbal and, physical trauma or if it were the sure signs of my life unravelling by a thread. I used to be so full of life. Now, I welcomed the thought of death. Lately, I had not been feeling like myself. I was used to being regarded as an independent, beautiful woman and making my own decisions based on what was best for Ellie and me. Our home used to be filled with an awesome reverence and the fear of God. These days, one would be hard pressed to find any signs of God within these walls. I had not been back to church in several months. I desperately missed my Sunday School class. My Pastor and church members were constantly calling and wondering about our well-being. The calls always went unanswered because I was not "allowed" to speak with anyone unless Broderick said it was acceptable. How did my life come to this?

Sadly, I was frequently made to feel as if Ellie and I were "in the wrong" for initially having a good solid foundation within our own home. Our once rock-solid routine had become completely non-existent. Broderick was very controlling and extremely harsh. He was adamant that I spent too much money on myself and also Ellie. My husband left us very well off and it was my responsibility to make sure that she continued to benefit from the hard work and dedication that my husband displayed when he was alive. He also said that I was "disrespecting him" by not spending enough time with him.

He felt like if I could go out and get manicures and pedicures that he needed to be treated like a "king" as well. He made unreasonable demands such as demanding personal pedicures in the middle of the night which he signalled that he was ready for by barging into the room and shouting, Come do my feet!". This meant that his feet were to be washed, massaged and scrubbed until *he* said that they were done correctly. The whole ridiculous process involved using my good jet spa foot tub, getting down on my hands and knees, and scraping his nasty feet with my good pedicure tools. I had originally purchased these items during a cruise excursion. It looked and felt ridiculous. I felt degraded.

During the times that he would stay away from the house (in my car) for hours at a time with no word of when he would return, he demanded that I make sure that a hot meal was waiting for him. It didn't make a difference if it were 5pm or 3:11 am – he expected a fully home cooked hot meal to be waiting on him. If not, I could expect another broken bone.

To make matters worse, I hadn't been "able" to speak with or see my three best friends in months. The day that we were set to leave on our International trip several months ago, he went into an awful rage. He broke my nose. Yes, he went ballistic because I would be leaving for so many consecutive days and he was not able to go. I explained to him repeatedly that this was a girl's trip. We planned it months in advance before I ever even met him! Even though I had recently lost my job (due to his frequent unexpected, angry appearances), I was still planning on taking my girls' trip. He was afraid that my friends would question my newly adopted lifestyle. There was a very present fear that his abusive ways would be discovered. He truly had me isolated.

Instead of my home being a place of peace and the love of Jesus Christ, you could almost see an invisible sign that read "Den of Iniquity" hanging over my front door. Broderick made the habit of taking my car to pick up his "friends" and bringing them back to my house to have parties, drink, smoke and play cards or dominos until the twilight hours. It was hard to sleep, and it made me uncomfortable. As you may remember, Ellie suffered from asthma. There were so many smoke-filled parties within my home, that our entire home, including the walls, drapes, carpet and custom upholstered furnishings smelled like a smoke-filled night club. Just last week, Ellie had to be taken to the emergency room for an asthma attack. I am sure it was due to these impromptu parties. I couldn't be exactly sure, but one day Ellie and I came home to what

66

smelled like marijuana. I was afraid to question him about it. I turned a blind eye.

I had grown tired of wearing my hair in a ponytail. I was no longer allowed to continue with my bi-weekly hair appointments. I had not visited the nail salon in weeks either. It was not that it was absolutely necessary, but I worked hard. I saved my money and paid my bills in a timely fashion for years. I was accustomed to this lifestyle. My hair was falling out in clumps and my nails were quite brittle. I suffered from a thyroid condition and I desperately needed my labs drawn and a refill on my medications. I was not allowed to see my Physician for fear that they would discover the abuse. Now, I was forced to give all of my money to him. I had lost my job because of him. But I was receiving a weekly unemployment check. To keep the peace, I just cashed them and gave the proceeds to him. This would buy me a few hours of peace and quiet.

There were numerous times that Broderick went through my wallet and had a field day with loose cash and his choice of credit cards. By the fifth month of his shenanigans, all four of my cards were maxed out. My credit score dropped from 789 to 435 according to Equifax. Both TransUnion and Experian were even lower than this. My cell phone was constantly ringing off the hook with calls from bill collectors. I was certainly not accustomed to this. After all, my husband and I had facilitated money management classes together at the local Community College. I thought to myself, "Jesus, I need you to be a financial planner for me right now." There were stacks of unpaid bills scattered throughout the house. This level of irresponsibility left me without a sense of financial or emotional stability. I was lost.

Ellie had started wetting the bed. She cried a great deal of the time. She no longer wanted to stay here. Truth be told, neither did I. My spirit had grown so weary that I contemplated just packing a suitcase for my sweet baby girl and I – and just walking away from everything. I had tried to leave so many times before. Each time I tried to leave him or force him to leave, he would make another attempt to discredit my story. The police had been called to the address so many times that I had lost count. My neighbors no longer spoke to me. When I pulled into my drive-way they would pretend that they did not see me waving at them. They no longer invited us over for family night or neighbourhood holiday parties. I was lonely.

I had once taken great pride in clipping fresh flowers for my vanity each week. I continued to do this one act of self-care until one day he asked who kept buying flowers for me every week. I assured him that no one was buying them. I explained that the one thing that I have left for myself that he hadn't destroyed was garden in the backyard. He quietly left the room. A few moments later, I heard a knock at the en suite bathroom window. He was standing outside of the window close to the perimeter of my flower garden. My garden contained beautiful flowers a set of beautiful purple tulips that my husband purchased and planted for me one year. He was standing very close to the edge of the flower bed. He smiled and showed those now devilishly pearly white teeth as he unzipped his pants and proudly urinated on my purple tulips. My husband had planted those tulips for me. I stood motionless as I looked him directly in the eyes. One single teardrop ran down my face. In one last act of evil, he yelled out, "Hey, b***h do you still want these raggedy a** flowers… what's that you say?" He looked down at the tulips and lifted his Timberland Boot off the ground and let it back down with force right onto my precious tulips. His pants were still around his calves. He motioned his middle finger at me through the window. I am certain that my heart skipped a 16-count symphony worth of rhythmic beats.

It turns out, Broderick *never* really held a job the entire time that we knew one another. In fact, the packages that he was holding the day that we met were purchased with the stolen credit cards of another woman that he was seeing at the time. Additionally, his dream car was in fact, a Range Rover. But it was just that; a dream. He didn't have his own car, nor a stable place to live. This man had several children by at least five different women. I found out that he had actually never been married. So yeah, dead wife? She was non-existent. He made up this whole story just to play on my emotions. It is amazing to see the great lengths that he would go to so that he could manipulate and subsequently destroy me. Why didn't I take heed to the signs in the beginning? The red flags were waving all around. Yet, I never cared to pay them any attention. In the end, it would seemingly cost me my whole existence.

As I sat on the edge of my bed, I waited for him to return. I knew what would happen next. I was so frightened because I was just starting to feel better after the last time that he hit me in my chest. I was certain that I had broken a rib. I wasn't sure because I wasn't able to sneak away to the Urgent Care. He was going out in my car more and more. He had also placed a digital tracking device on my cell phone so that he could keep up with my minute to minute location, whether it was inside the house or out in the open community. He came into the house in an even greater rage! He came charging towards me and began to hit me in the back of my head repeatedly. He said that I kept doing things to set him off. He questioned whether I was doing these things on purpose or not. I never answered and I never moved. I had given up. I allowed him to do with me as he wished. He continued to pound into my skull with his closed fist. He often did this so that I wouldn't receive any visible bruises. I was starting to see stars dancing around. I finally shouted out "ENOUGH! ENOUGH! ENOUGH!!"

I turned around to look him directly in the eye. The blows kept coming and after so many punches, something came over me. I snapped! I quickly went from sitting on the edge of the bed to standing in the middle of mattress and trying desperately to defend myself. The sheets had been off the bed for almost a week because they were bloody and filled with stains from my last encounter with his fist. I did not have the energy to complete laundry. By this point, I had suffered at least 17 broken bones, a missing tooth and he had even tried (unsuccessfully) to cut my ponytail off while I lay sleeping. So, the pillow top mattress pockets gave me good traction as I fought to keep my balance. I was swinging carelessly and telling him to leave! I told him over and over to get out and never come back! Finally, one of the punches connected and hit him directly in the face. It left a large scratch. I think it surprised him because he just touched his face and looked and the scant amount of blood on his fingertips. He looked at me again and quietly left the room.

To my absolute surprise, he was sitting out on the porch steps. It had been almost an hour. Though I was thankful for a few moments of peace, the atmosphere was eerily quiet. I peeped out the front door window and realized that he was not simply sitting on the porch alone. He was sitting there with big crocodile tears rolling down his face…talking to a police officer. He had secretly called the police to report *me* for domestic violence. I thought I had seen it all! To make matters worse, it seemed as if the officer was sympathizing with him. I heard the officer say, "You know men are victims as well. It's ok to cry. Let it all out. We are here for you."

At that moment, a second officer came to the door in order to speak with me. I was hysterical before I could even open the door. I am standing here in the doorway of my own home, half dressed, with my hair all over my head and tears running down my face. I explained my side of the story and to my surprise, my next door neighbor came over to speak with the officer to vouch for my character. I asked the officer if they could please just make Broderick leave because we were not married and just wanted my life back. I told them about all of the horrible things that he had done to Ellie and I. When the officer asked to see Ellie to check on her safety. I lead them to her bedroom. To my surprise, it seemed that Ellie had slept through this entire ordeal.

I pleaded with the officers to make him leave. Since he had stayed within this home for greater than 6 months, they were legally unable to make him exit the home because legally, this was now his residence as well. All he had to do was produce evidence that he had items within the home that would serve as proof that this was a shared residence. Well, there was no problem there. His reason for taking my credit cards served a two-fold purpose. He was able to buy whatever he wanted, whenever he wanted. But he also knew from past experiences with these state laws that if law enforcement were called, he would need to make sure that he could produce evidence that this was a shared residence. Check mate.

Once the police left the premises, I was met with the familiar sound of his almost demonic screams echoing throughout the walls of my home. He taunted and teased me. He told me that no one would ever believe my story. He went on to arrogantly explain how Ellie had witnessed him "putting that kid at the Pizzeria in his place" all those months ago, and he was certain that she never told a soul. He let me know that neither she nor I was smart enough to escape his tight grip. He smiled sarcastically. Then he proceeded to let me know that I could try to make him leave if I wanted to, but if he couldn't have me then no one would. His award winning, pearly white teeth suddenly disappeared behind his dry, cracked and bleeding lips. I was sickened by his appearance. He never shaved nor kept his hair cut anymore. Bathing seemed to be completely optional these days for him. I was nauseated and sickened at his very appearance.

Before this Armageddon like final battle was able to commence, I told him under no uncertain terms that I wanted him gone! His simple reply was that he would leave, but it would be only after stepping over the threshold of my dead body. An almost demon possessed rage came over Broderick as he whispered, "Prepare to die b***h!"

My response was even colder. You could hear something inside of me crack. A shift had taken place within my body and it started from the depths of my soul. I did not flinch. I just looked at him with a hateful, cold and calculating death stare and told him that I was finished being his punching bag. I was taking my life back and I meant it! I told Broderick that Ellie and I were leaving and when we get back, he had better be gone! I reached my hand into his pocket and removed my house key and car keys and placed them into my shoulder bag. I was tired. We were going to be free once and for all. I placed Ellie in my arms. She buried her little head into my shoulder. I held onto her tightly. "Prince Charming" tried to block the doorway so that we couldn't escape. I pushed him out of my way with my free arm and tried desperately to make our escape.

Just as I turned the doorknob to lead Ellie and I out to the car, I felt him grab the back of my shirt collar. He told me that I wasn't going anywhere. He started to choke my neck from behind and eventually he forced me to the floor. He pulled the leather straps clean off my Coach purse and caused me to fall backwards onto Ellie. My heartbeat was tachycardiac and unsettling. An extreme sense of fear was trying to overtake me. I was crying uncontrollably by this point. I didn't want my sweet Ellie to witness the horrendous scene that was playing out right before her eyes. So, I gathered enough strength and told Ellie to run. I wanted my dear Ellie to run as fast as she could. She didn't deserve this front row seat to the final battle between this monster who was attempting to take her mother's life. I repeatedly yelled at her to run…just run!

My body is drawn into a lifeless ball. My small, previously confident silhouette has been transformed into a helpless heap of flesh. I am unable to successfully remove myself from a fetal position. I fear that my very spirit has met the threshold of final disappointment. His last strike to my face caused me to stumble clumsily just across the living room threshold. My spirit seems to have left my body. I find myself hovering above my former self. I seem to be lifeless. My ears remain open, as well as my eyes. It's hard to blink. I can't stop the tears from falling. But there is no longer the sound of a whimpering cry. I am tired. My body has returned itself, involuntarily, to what was once a place of safety. In this position I feel safe. While in this position my head hangs increasingly lower. The quiet confident arch in my back has decreased its once feminine delicate nature into that of a wounded animal. I have bowed heavily to fear. If you were to gaze upon my limbs, you would see that they now intersect close to my heart. Maybe this is symbolic of my desperate need for protection. Perhaps God will hear my cry and give me the gift of his eternal safe embrace. At any rate, I have been deceived for the last time. I feel as if it would be easier to surrender rather than continue the battle.

Ellie was so terrified at what she was witnessing that she just stood there frozen. During the struggle, the contents of my purse has scattered across the slick marble floor. Ellie stood there watching "Prince Charming" continuously kick me in my back and punch me repeatedly as I screamed out in excruciating pain after each blow. Ellie watched as one of the closed fist punches caused a streak of blood to fly several feet across the foyer. Ellie and I made eye contact for what would be the last time. I looked at her through tear filled eyes and said quietly through my blood-stained teeth, "Run baby. Please run." Then, I prayed a silent prayer that God would protect my baby. I was sure that my life would soon be over.

Ellie ran to the little doorway that was situated under the staircase. It was a little secret door that her father had created for her, so that she could play with her dolls and read her books. There was just enough room for a little pillow, a flashlight and a picture of Ellie, her dad and I. It had been a while since Ellie played inside her secret hideaway. Life was very different for her these days. Despite the sheer chaos, endless screaming and persistent crying that she heard going on in the other room, I imagine that she suddenly felt safe. Before running into the secret hideaway, Ellie picked up her mother's broken purse, the keys and her cell phone. There was a very small circular opening at the edge of the tiny sliding door. She placed her eye against the circle and tried to see if she could see her mommy. She started to cry quietly as she witnessed the sounds of glass objects breaking over and over.

Ellie heard her mother scream rather loudly that her hand was bleeding! She was screaming out in a level of pain that seemed totally unbearable. She kept screaming "I'm bleeding out! Please...stop!" Ellie remembered how earlier that day the police officer did not believe her mommy's story. She was so hurt by this. As it turns out, Ellie had not slept through the previous encounter. She was wide awake, but she remained quiet when the police came to their home. Ellie had become so accustomed to visits from police that it was almost drilled into her to go into her room and remain there for safety.

Ellie heard the sound of something bumping into the wall and it sounded like furniture was moving all around. There was also the continuous sound of glass breaking. In between the breaking glass and pounding of walls that signified the great struggle, little Ellie started to silently cry. She was very afraid so she decided to see if she could call someone for help from her mother's cell phone. Out of extreme desperation, Ellie took her mother's phone to try to call her grandparents for help. She wasn't quite sure how to make a phone call, because she couldn't read that well yet. So, she started to push any button that she could find. One of the buttons that she pushed was the speed dial number to her Auntie Bentley. When Bentley answered the phone, she was met with the cries for help from her niece Ellie. Bentley kept screaming "Hello? Ellie, where are you? Where is your mother?" Ellie wondered if her Aunt Bentley would believe her story. Ellie had become so scared that she dropped the phone. The call disconnected.

Ellie was determined to help her mother. She knew that no one would understand what she was trying to tell them. But Ellie thought about one of her favorite times of the week in kindergarten called "show and tell" Ellie thought about all of the many times that her mother had taken her to amusement parks, library puppet shows and exciting theme parks. She remembered how her mommy would hit a little blue button on her phone and then say, "We are live Ellie!" She didn't really understand how it all worked, but she figured it was worth a try. Ellie hit the little blue button with the letter "F" and looked at the screen. She could read well enough to see that the top corner of the screen said "Live." Ellie began to immediately pour her heart out. Her tearful, desperately revealed plea for help went something like this:

"Hi. My name is Ellie and I'm five years old. Can you please help us? My mommy is crying… and she is hurting really bad. I am here at home hiding under the stairs from the mean man that keeps hitting my mommy. There is glass breaking. He keeps yelling. Mommy is crying really bad." Ellie heard another very loud crash that was coming from the living room. It sounded like something hit the large glass and metal table. (In the background, the very sounds that she was experiencing were also clearly audible to whomever may have been listening.) Ellie went on to explain that her mommy taught her to always tell the truth, so she wanted to do a "show and tell" session because Mr. Broderick said that no one would believe me if I ever told on him. Ellie went onto say, "I am hiding under the stairs but don't tell Mr Broderick where I am if you come over. Ellie started crying even harder and said, "Please, anybody…we just need a little help." Ellie went on to explain how Mr. Broderick yelled a lot and hit her mommy almost every day. She went on to explain how her mommy looked really bad and she was breathing really funny. Ellie made it know that she was quite scared. Ellie began to explain how Mr. Broderick kept buying her mommy flowers. She described how the same vase kept getting filled with different flowers. Mommy didn't like flowers anymore. Ellie explained that the water in the vase was dirty and smelly now. She went on to explain that the flowers used to be bright purple like jelly beans. But now the petals had fallen off and died. She said that if someone could come and save them, she would buy her mommy some flowers to make her feel better.

She ended by saying "My address is 3-5-8-3 Petals View Court because that's what mommy taught me in case of an emergency. This seems like an emergency, so it's okay tell you where I live! I hope you can find us soon." Then she added, "I know that God will send help, because mommy always says that God promised to take care of us." Ellie laid the phone down, but she neglected to turn the live stream off. It turns out that there were 648 live viewers who had watched and shared the post multiple times. Ellie wanted her Otie bear. But she was too afraid to come out. Mommy told her to hide and so that is just what she did.

Ellie heard one final scream from her mother. The fight had moved throughout the house and ended up at the foyer close to the staircase. It sounded like she was close to the bottom of the stairs. "Prince Charming" stepped over her body and proceeded to step violently through the house shouting that he was looking for Ellie. He said that when he found her, she would be sorry. He went on a rant stating that she was becoming a tiny annoyance. He expressed that he hated her, and he hated her room! Several times, he expressed his indwelling hate for Ellie's deceased father. He hated anything that was a reminder of her father's.

Suddenly, the smell of fresh paint was extremely overpowering. He had taken the remaining paint from the office and commenced to throwing it all over Ellie's bedroom from ceiling to floor. The curtains and the bed that Ellie's father had originally placed in her room (which used to be her nursery) were now destroyed. Ellie's little bike with the training wheels was sitting over in the corner of her bedroom. He went over to where it was sitting and with his bare hands ripped the loose screws out of the wheels. He stormed into the hallway and threw the training wheels and they landed just in front of the little door where Ellie was hiding.

The training wheels on Ellie's bike were always so special to her. Her dad was teaching her how to ride a bike and one of the last requests that Ellie made before he died was to keep the training wheels on. When her father asked why, she explained to him that she felt safe with them on. She said that it felt like he was still holding her up while they were on. So, the moment that Ellie saw what this real-life monster had done, she became extremely upset. But she knew she had to continue to wait quietly in case someone saw her message and came to help. Ellie's mother was breathing with great difficulty. She heard her mother seemingly talking to someone and saying the names of colors. Ellie didn't understand what exactly was happening. But she continued to remain quiet.

Suddenly, there was a loud crash that came from one of the bedroom windows. He had taken Ellie's bicycle and thrown it clear through the window and into the back yard. He was yelling and cursing throughout the entire ordeal. You could hear him turn over furniture and throwing books and even toys through the newly broken window. He turned around and saw that Ellie's favorite teddy bear was wearing her deceased father's favorite college t-shirt. He picked up the bear, closed his eyes and commenced to ripping the shirt off of her precious bear. He picked up the shirt and used it to smear the fresh paint into the walls. He did so as he laughed like a new age version of Dr Jekyll and Mr. Hyde. He pulled the stuffing out of the bear and ripped the remaining button-shaped eye off Otie's little face. Ellie's favorite reminder of her father's love had been destroyed.

"Therefore, we do not lose heart. Even though our outward man is perishing, yet the inward man is being renewed day by day." - 2 Corinthians 4:16

Chapter 9

He Loves Me Not

*P*urple. Red. Black. These are the three descriptive words that she uttered to the 911 dispatcher to describe the last recollection of what she saw as she received the devastating physical blow to her already withered, feeble body. Her vision has been hindered by the free-flowing blood that is running from her forehead. As she attempts to lift herself from the floor, a piece of glass that was once a part of a beautiful wedding goblet had sliced her finger quite deep. There was so much irony to this. A beautiful gift from the happiest day of her life with her now deceased husband, was now responsible for a horrendous injury on what would prove to be one of the darkest days of her life. The amount of blood loss as a result of her numerous physical injuries is unfathomable. These injuries would surely require countless stitches and painful surgical correction. She was just starting to heal from the last series of bruises and visible wounds on her arms and back.

In her head, she doesn't have the stable reasoning to realize that she will not have a choice but to take a ride in the ambulance to the hospital. She had been badly wounded before, but the severity of her injuries this time, were by far, the most brutal and intense. In her confusion, she wonders what the urgent care Physicians will say and will she even live long enough to make it to seek help? Prayerfully, it won't be as painful as the last time. The urgent care staff had become so familiar with her visits, that they would often times whisper amongst themselves at her arrival. The frequency of her visits had become greater as time passed. And, the severity of the injuries became even more gruesome.

The living room is a hopeless, bloody disaster zone. The amount of broken glass and blood-stained carpet looks strikingly similar to climactic scenes out of a criminal investigation program on a popular cable television series. Each time she tries to lift her head, all she can see are the purple spots dancing around her like little dragon flies. She is pulling herself through a sea of broken glass. Her elbows are too weak to hold the weight of her battered frame as she pulls herself to the stairs. The carpeted stair case was lined with the remnants of damaged picture frames that once held photos of happy memories. "Fourteen" she whispered quietly. This is the total number of stairs that she would have to somehow climb in order to make it to the "safety" of her bedroom. It was the closest room that had a sturdy lock. She knew that it took several minutes for paramedics to arrive. They had visited their address on numerous occasions. It was almost a rite of passage for the weekend. They were on a first name basis by this time. She knew that it was safer for Ellie to remain hidden under the secret stairway passage.

The ringing in her ears is so loud that it is almost deafening. Her breathing is hurried and there is a harsh, crackling congestion strongly accompanying each inhalation of air. Every passing breath was more difficult than the last. The last three ribs are poking downward into her abdomen almost like a thorn in her side. She begins to ask herself if it is even worth trying to save herself from this monster. She placed her hand onto the handrail and used the last bit of strength in her body to pull herself up the seemingly insurmountable staircase. In painful desperation, her tears cry for peace and her soul cries out to God for help.

On each step that she mounted, there was a souvenir of the events that had taken place. On the first step, there was a broken figurine that her mother had given her as a gift when she moved out on her own for the very first time. She was holding her wounded rib cage tightly to ease the difficulty in breathing as she attempted to place her bent and broken body onto the second stair. She rested her head softly on the edge of the wall adjacent to the second stair. The congestion and blood curdling cough were becoming increasingly noticeable. There on the second stair she saw her broken key fob to her car. She slowly wiped the glass and plaster dust away from the surface. There was a large hole in the wall as a result of the previous struggle on the staircase. She leans her head back in exhaustion. She begins to weep uncontrollably. Her hands, face, legs and feet are covered with blood. Due to the length of the struggle, some wounds are beginning to clot while others are persistently bleeding freely.

As she peers out of her tired, sunken eyes over into the open-air living space, she notices that the once clean and crisp contemporary surroundings are now reduced to what appears to be a pretentious war zone. The wall to wall carpet looks as if it was the setting of a biblical time sacrifice. The beautifully arranged coffee table books are now broken at the spine, missing jacket covers and riddled with torn pages. The familiar artsy, rounded glass table that once served as the eye-catching centrepiece of the room, was subsequently used as a wrestling mat that would intensify the damage of her backwards fall. Her efforts to escape the vile hands of this monster were numerous and unsettling. This conversation piece is now reduced to a scattered disarray of broken glass chards and a bent metal frame. The beautiful custom designed living room furniture was once a place of retreat and relaxation. The level of destruction and chaos was far worse than the aftermath of the 2010 flood. Love could not possibly live here. It could never have resided in between these walls.

Questions torment and multiply in her mind. Why did she continue to lose herself at the hands of this abuser? Why not just give up the ghost? The one thing that kept her fighting this battle was her child. She knew that she had to be there for her precious daughter. She gave her a reason to live. Her daughter's loving spirit and kindness, despite their dire circumstances, gave her the strength to hold on. For this reason, she knew that giving up was not an option.

When dealing with an abuser, you must be aware of your surroundings at all costs. She realizes that the condo is brimming with an extremely eerie stillness. She remembers glass crashing into walls and the distant sound of windows breaking. There are no signs of the abuser in sight. She seems to have lost all concept of time by this point. Had she been bleeding an hour? Two hours? How much time had passed since she had called 911? Why wasn't anyone coming to help her? She slowly moved her head so that she could fix her gaze onto her cell phone in her housecoat pocket. What were all of these buttons? She slowly lifted the cell phone to see if she could get a dial tone. Shades of purple, red and black flash as she muttered "Hello?" into the phone. Her mind and spirit seemed so broken and uncomprehensive, that it was not a phone, in fact, it was a remote control. She slowly realized that in the initial struggle, Ellie had taken her phone with her to hide.

Suddenly, the floors rumbled uncontrollably, and the walls shook mightily. The sound of rattling window panes was overpowering. She heard a distorted jingle of metal with each boom. She laid empty and tired, still on the second step of the staircase, when she noticed the detached spare car key was inches away from her face. She inhaled sharply, as she knew she wouldn't make it to the third step. He burst through the door and locked his eyes on the spare key and snatched it. She looked at him frightened and pleaded with the last few breaths she had. "Please no…" He angrily drew his arm back and violently rammed his fist into her face. He stormed down the hallway, stating that he was looking for his gun. He said that he was going to finish her off once and for all. He kicked her in the head violently one last time. He left her there in a pool of her own blood and urine. She lost all bodily function, as well as her will to survive. Her entire world crumbled as her remaining vision faded to black. The last words that whispered were "I love you Ellie." She never made it to the third stair.

"Prince Charming" was moving through the house violently cursing and tearing the house apart looking for his gun. He was frantically going through each room of the house leaving a trail as he went. He stormed through the hallway pulling sheets and towels out of the linen closet. He knocked over the china cabinet and curio that was situated in the dining room. Glass went flying everywhere. Then he went to the foyer in search of his gun. I never had a clue that the gun was there in plain sight this whole time. The question is, what if Ellie had gotten hold of it?

He pulled out the top drawer of the foyer entryway table. In the process he knocked over the glass vase that was filled with the old stagnant water and purple "forgive me" flowers. He slowly reached under the vase to obtain the key to the gun box. Then, he reached into the drawer and pulled out his firearm. As I glanced up into the mirror over the foyer table, I saw the cold and calculated look on his face. It was the grimacing look of a serial killer. He cocked the gun and turned around swiftly to fire. He pulled his finger back on the trigger to fire!

Just then, a loud boom resounded throughout the foyer. The smoke from the gun was still rising from the weapon chamber as the gun fell to the floor. The front door had been knocked clean off the hinges with great ease. The door hit "Prince Charming" on the back of the head and with the hard fall, he sustained a slight gash to his back of his head. As he slowly dropped to the floor, the broken door fell to the ground and with it, you could hear the sound of several pairs of boot laced footsteps stepping over the endless sea of broken glass and picture frames with a resounding cadence. Six men in leather motorcycle jackets and sunglasses stood intentional watch over his motionless body as they waited for the authorities to arrive. They were dear friends of Ellie's father. They belonged to the same charity motorcycle club.

A seventh man came in and with a very familiar male voice shouted, "Ellie, where are you baby?" It was another one of Ellie's uncles from her father's charity motorcycle club. As it turns out, the resounding boom was not close-range gunfire, but it was one of Ellie's forever uncles kicking in the front door! The rattling of the walls and windows that was previously heard was the sound of this army of motorcycle angels coming to rescue Ellie and her mother. He and the other members of this wonderful army of motorcycle angels came pouring into the door to rescue them. These men had promised one another that they would never allow harm to come to their wives or children. Brotherhood was taken seriously amongst them, in life and even in death. Though Ellie's father was no longer with them, he lived on through her forever uncles as she called them. Ellie was peeping through the tiny hole in the triangular sliding door and shouted, "Here I am Uncle Dee-Dee! He kneeled down and carefully slid the door open and staring back at him were a pair of tear-filled yet brave appearing brown eyes. He bent lower to pick her up and hold her in his arms. Her Uncle Dee-Dee told her that everything would be ok. And she *believed* him.

To her surprise, they had all been watching the Facebook live stream this entire time…and, so had the rest of the world. After a total of over 1,000 shares there was no question that the world was watching and certainly believed the story. There was not a question; this coward had to be stopped!

Uncle Jonathan and Uncle Peter rushed to assist Ellie's mother. They were both medics in the armed services. They reassured her that help was on the way. Each of them pleaded with her to hold on a little while longer. As they were waiting patiently with Ellie's mother, she heard the sound of high heels click clacking across the foyer floor. She knew that familiar sound. The hurried cadence of heels was none other than her Aunties Bentley, Rayna and Pamela. They rushed to the stairway to comfort their friend. They didn't say a word. They sat with her until help arrived.

In the distance you could hear the ambulance sirens wailing and the glaring of police sirens was a loudly overwhelming yet welcoming sound. There was even a local television station van pulled into the cul de sac. Just like God promised, he sent help. Ellie remembers saying that God would keep his promises, just like her mother always taught her. And He did just that.

The police arrived and took this violent monster into custody. There were no questions asked. The only verbal interaction with this man was his rights being read as he was being given first aid for the gash he had suffered during the struggle at the front door. It was all broadcasted live by a brilliant, little girl that simply wanted to be honest and play "show and tell." She wanted to show what was happening to she and her mommy. She just wanted her mommy to be okay. God promised to take care of them. God was faithful to keep His promise.

May I tell you the rest of the story in my own words? I can truly say that I am no longer a victim. I am a survivor. As you may have noticed, I never revealed my name through the entire story. As I shared this story, I wanted you to see the objective signs of trauma and abuse without placing the stigma of a name or face along with this horrible epidemic. I am every woman. My story represents the millions of women across the globe who do not have a voice. You may be in the presence of a friend, co worker or family member that may be dealing with this horrible epidemic. So, this is the reason I chose not to reveal my name in this story. The events could be interchangeable with part of your story. The lowest common denominator is the presence of abuse and destructive behavioural patterns. My story could easily be your story.

I know what it feels like to allow your guard down in the heat of passion and find yourself attached at the hip with a seemingly never-ending cycle of dysfunction and pain. Every part of my world was crumbling before my eyes, but God met me at the point of my greatest need. He covered me when I truly didn't deserve His grace and mercy.

Due to the unannounced visits and fits of rage at my place of employment, I lost my job during this horrible dilemma. I almost lost my sweet daughter during this horrific time. I watched as she reverted back to wetting the bed, suffering from nightmares and inability to stay asleep throughout the night. Ellie didn't deserve any of this horrible treatment. She was an innocent bystander throughout this entire horrible dilemma. She was confused, sad and felt abandoned. I never thought about it prior to this – but Ellie could have easily become an orphan child had I died on that dreadful day. But again, God's grace and mercy rushed into our home like a river. We had not experienced this level of peace and compassion within those four walls for a very long time. I am still not sure how I went from walking with Christ and having the desire to live like him, to willingly dancing with the devil to the tune of impending death and destruction.

Three full weeks have passed since that dreadful day. Today will be our first day home since I was transported to the hospital. My parents drove us home from the hospital and I received word that my homegirls, in keeping with our lifetime theme of sisterhood to one another, were almost done cleaning the house in anticipation of our arrival. Our story of triumph was being shared through social media to people across the world. But what if Ellie had not shared the story on that dreadful day? What about the times when women are battered and abused each day and they are left to be the only witness to their silent cry for help? What about all the incidents that go unreported for fear of retaliation and further abandonment? I am most thankful to the Lord above for his tender mercies towards Ellie and me.

As we got out of the car and walked onto the porch, a sense of peace that we had not experienced in a very long time met us at the front door. When we entered, the scent of fresh laundry and potpourri greeted us with a kiss. The carpets looked to have been professionally cleaned and the broken glass had been removed. Over the course of several weeks, Ellie's forever Uncles pitched in and repaired her window, hung new curtains and even repaired her bed. We are not sure how they did it, but there was not a drop of paint left in sight from that terrible incident. They got together and purchased Ellie and new bike, just like the one her father gave her for Christmas.

They even placed the old training wheels onto this new bike. As for Otie, they weren't able to find Ellie another one to replace the one that she lost. So, her grandmother pulled out her sewing kit and repaired him so well that you would have that a professional seamstress was on deck! I had one more of her dad's college t-shirts in the closet, so we decided that we would place it on Otie to keep him warm.

As we stood in the entry way, we took a few moments to look at how fresh and new the entire household seemed. The only remnant of the former state of affairs was the purple flowers poking out from the top of the Waterford crystal vase that still contained the last set of "I'm sorry" roses from "Prince Charming." They had continued to wither during our time away. Ellie stood there and watched as I pulled out the very last long stem purple rose from the vase. I looked intently at the dried, faded petals and began to pick the remaining petals off at the stem and then I softly said, "He loves me...he loves me not...he loves me...he loves me not...he loves me...he loves me not." Each petal fell to the ground carelessly. The color had left the petals and there was not moisture nor life that could easily be traced within the petals. I smiled and took a deep breath as I was ready to walk into our fresh, new start.

As I placed the remaining stem along the top of the foyer table, Ellie bent down to pick up one lone petal. She looked at me with her big brown eyes and said, "Mommy look!" To my surprise, it was a purple rose petal. It was full of life and looked as if it were never without water. The petal was strong despite the conditions of the other petals around it. It appeared to be full of life. I looked towards the heavens clutching the purple petal and whispered, "He loves me."

At that moment, I realized that God had never taken his hand from me. He still loved me! This is much like the story of the potter's wheel and the clay. Life may be moving forward at dizzying speeds and it may seem as if our footing is about to slip. But while the potter is forming the clay on his wheel, he is so very careful to allow his hands to remain firmly planted upon the clay to secure the piece that is being formed. He never wants to see His masterpiece fall away and be broken. This is the reason for keeping a steady hand on His creation.

God truly wants the very best for His children. He leaves evidence of His mighty presence all around us. How ironic that these faded purple roses were a reminder of the tremendous battle that had just taken place not many weeks ago. Today, I am standing in my home and it feels as if the atmosphere has shifted to the welcoming, familiar place that Ellie and I were accustomed to. As I looked at the beauty of the purple rose petal that seems to have survived against all odds, it reminds me of the promises of God for my life.

When the world was destroyed by flood in the days of Noah, God sent a rainbow that would serve as a covenant reminder that God would not allow the world to be destroyed by water again. The colors of the rainbow also had great significance as related to this promise. No one is able to undo the completed work of the cross! It does not matter what you have experienced or what you are going through, God's work is a completed work. His promises are still good. The rainbow may be looked upon as a complete picture of Jesus Christ.

Rainbow Spectrum: Purple, Blue, Green, Yellow, Orange and Red.

Purple stands for Royalty. I am from a royal priesthood through the blood of Jesus. It makes no difference what names I have been called or what people think of me, I am Royalty because of my heavenly Father. When I look at this purple petal, I am filled with a sense of hope for the future. I no longer have to fall prey to fear. This purple petal is my story. I was existing amongst many self-inflicted situations that could be thought of as prickly thorns. At first it was beautiful and then it became unbearable to look upon. But, through it all God left a sign to let me know that I am who HE says that I am. Thank you for your loving kindness God! *Blue* stands for the heavenlies. It is the place where Jesus is seated at the right hand of His Father. God sits high and looks down low. *Green* is significant of new life. I am thankful for a second chance at life. *Yellow* stands for not only sunlight but SON light – for Jesus is truly the light of the world. *Orange* is the warning light that reminds us to turn from our sinful ways and repent. *Red* represents the blood of Jesus that causes us to be washed whiter than snow. I offer Christ to you, right now. He is standing willing and able to comfort, lead and guide you. He is waiting to accept you with open arms. God is waiting to send healing and make you whole again. He loves you.

Appendix

The information in the following pages was strategically placed in this section to decrease the likelihood of an abuser realizing that this book is not a novel, but more of a survivor's manual. In the following pages you will find helpful definitions and abundant resources concerning domestic violence. Used by permission. All rights reserved.

Section I - What is Domestic Violence
Section II - Who Can Be in an Abusive Relationship?
Section III – Type of Abuse
Section IV – Safety Plans
Section V - Leaving a Relationship
Section VI – National Domestic Violence Resources by State

What Is Domestic Violence?

Does your partner ever....

- Insult, demean or embarrass you with put-downs?
- Control what you do, who you talk to or where you go?
- Look at you or act in ways that scare you?
- Push you, slap you, choke you or hit you?
- Stop you from seeing your friends or family members?
- Control the money in the relationship? Take your money or Social Security check, make you ask for money or refuse to give you money?
- Make all of the decisions without your input or consideration of your needs?
- Tell you that you're a bad parent or threaten to take away your children?
- Prevent you from working or attending school?
- Act like the abuse is no big deal, deny the abuse or tell you it's your own fault?
- Destroy your property or threaten to kill your pets?
- Intimidate you with guns, knives or other weapons?
- Attempt to force you to drop criminal charges?
- Threaten to commit suicide, or threaten to kill you?

If you answered 'yes' to even one of these questions, you may be in an unhealthy or abusive relationship. In this section, you'll find more information on the types of abuse, why people abuse and why it's so difficult to leave. Don't hesitate to chat or call the National Domestic Violence Hotline at (1-800-799-7233) if anything you read raises a red flag about your own relationship or that of someone you know. You may also visit their website at https://www.thehotline.org

Abuse Defined
Domestic violence can happen to anyone of any race, age, sexual orientation, religion or gender. How is it defined?

Why Do People Abuse?
Abuse is about power and control.

Why Do People Stay in Abusive Relationships?
If you've never been in an abusive relationship, it's hard to understand why it's so difficult to leave.

LGBTQ Abuse
Victims of domestic violence in the LGBTQ communities often experience abuse in ways that are specific and unique to these communities.

Abuse and Immigrants
Everyone has the right to live life free of abuse. Immigrants in the US may have specific concerns about getting help.

What is a Healthy Relationship?
What does a "healthy" relationship look like? In a relationship, who decides what is healthy and what isn't?

Domestic violence (also called intimate partner violence (IPV), domestic abuse or relationship abuse) is a pattern of behaviors used by one partner to maintain power and control over another partner in an intimate relationship.

Domestic violence does not discriminate. Anyone of any race, age, sexual orientation, religion or gender can be a victim – or perpetrator – of domestic violence. It can happen to people who are married, living together or who are dating. It affects people of all socioeconomic backgrounds and education levels.

Domestic violence includes behaviors that physically harm, arouse fear, prevent a partner from doing what they wish or force them to behave in ways they do not want. It includes the use of physical and sexual violence, threats and intimidation, emotional abuse and economic deprivation. Many of these different forms of domestic violence/abuse can be occurring at any one time within the same intimate relationship.

Why Do People Abuse?

Domestic violence and abuse stem from a desire to gain and maintain power and control over an intimate partner. Abusive people believe they have the right to control and restrict their partners, and they may enjoy the feeling that exerting power gives them. They often believe that their own feelings and needs should be the priority in their relationships, so they use abusive tactics to dismantle equality and make their partners feel less valuable and deserving of respect in the relationship.

No matter why it happens, abuse is not okay, and it's never justified.

Abuse is a learned behavior. Sometimes people see it in their own families. Other times they learn it from friends or popular culture. However, abuse is a choice, and it's not one that anyone has to make. Many people who experience or witness abuse growing up decide not to use those negative and hurtful ways of behaving in their own relationships. While outside forces such as drug or alcohol addiction can sometimes escalate abuse, it's most important to recognize that these issues do not cause abuse.

Who Can Be in an Abusive Relationship?

Anyone can be abusive, and anyone can be the victim of abuse. It happens regardless of gender, age, sexual orientation, race or economic background. If you are being abused by your partner, you may feel confused, afraid, angry and/or trapped. All of these emotions are normal responses to abuse. You might also blame yourself for what is happening. But no matter what others might say, you are never responsible for your partner's abusive actions. Being abusive is a choice. It's a strategic behavior the abusive person uses to create their desired power dynamic. Regardless of the circumstances of the relationship or the pasts of either partner, *no one ever deserves to be abused.*

At The Domestic Violence Hotline, they use the **Power & Control Wheel*** to describe most accurately what occurs in an abusive relationship.

Think of the wheel as a diagram of the tactics an abusive partner uses to keep their victim in the relationship. While the inside of the wheel is comprised of subtle, continual behaviors, the outer ring represents physical, visible violence. These are the abusive acts that are more overt and forceful, and often the intense acts that reinforce the regular use of other more subtle methods of abuse.

*Although this Power & Control Wheel uses she/her pronouns for the victim and assumes a male perpetrator, abuse can happen to people of any gender in any type of relationship.

<u>*T*ypes of Abuse</u>

Physical

You may be experiencing physical abuse if your partner has done or repeatedly does any of the following tactics of abuse:

- Pulling your hair, punching, slapping, kicking, biting or choking you
- Forbidding you from eating or sleeping
- Hurting you with weapons
- Preventing you from calling the police or seeking medical attention
- Harming your children
- Abandoning you in unfamiliar places
- Driving recklessly or dangerously when you are in the car with them
- Forcing you to use drugs or alcohol (especially if you've had a substance abuse problem in the past)

Emotional

You may be in an emotionally/verbally abusive relationship if you partner exerts control through:

- Calling you names, insulting you or continually criticizing you
- Refusing to trust you and acting jealous or possessive
- Trying to isolate you from family or friends
- Monitoring where you go, who you call and who you spend time with
- Demanding to know where you are every minute
- Trapping you in your home or preventing you from leaving
- Using weapons to threaten to hurt you
- Punishing you by withholding affection
- Threatening to hurt you, the children, your family or your pets
- Damaging your property when they're angry (throwing objects, punching walls, kicking doors, etc.)

- Humiliating you in any way
- Blaming you for the abuse
- Gaslighting
- Accusing you of cheating and being often jealous of your outside relationships
- Serially cheating on you and then blaming you for his or her behavior
- Cheating on you intentionally to hurt you and then threatening to cheat again
- Cheating to prove that they are more desired, worthy, etc. than you are
- Attempting to control your appearance: what you wear, how much/little makeup you wear, etc.
- Telling you that you will never find anyone better, or that you are lucky to be with a person like them.

Sexual

Sexually abusive methods of retaining power and control include an abusive partner:

- Forcing you to dress in a sexual way
- Insulting you in sexual ways or calls you sexual names
- Forcing or manipulating you into to having sex or performing sexual acts
- Holding you down during sex
- Demanding sex when you're sick, tired or after hurting you
- Hurting you with weapons or objects during sex
- Involving other people in sexual activities with you against your will
- Ignoring your feelings regarding sex
- Forcing you to watch pornography
- Purposefully trying to pass on a sexually transmitted disease to you

Sexual coercion

Sexual coercion lies on the 'continuum' of sexually aggressive behavior. It can vary from being egged on and persuaded, to being forced to have contact. It can be verbal and emotional, in the form of statements that make you feel pressure, guilt, or shame. You can also be made to feel forced through more subtle actions. For example, an abusive partner:

- Making you feel like you owe them — ex. Because you're in a relationship, because you've had sex before, because they spent money on you or bought you a gift
- Giving you drugs and alcohol to "loosen up" your inhibitions
- Playing on the fact that you're in a relationship, saying things such as: "Sex is the way to prove your love for me," "If I don't get sex from you, I'll get it somewhere else"
- Reacting negatively with sadness, anger or resentment if you say no or don't immediately agree to something
- Continuing to pressure you after you say no
- Making you feel threatened or afraid of what might happen if you say no
- Trying to normalize their sexual expectations: ex. "I need it, I'm a man"

Even if your partner isn't forcing you to do sexual acts against your will, being made to feel *obligated* is coercion in itself. Dating someone, being in a relationship, or being married never means that you *owe* your partner intimacy of any kind.

Reproductive Coercion

Reproductive coercion is a form of power and control where one partner strips the other of the ability to control their own reproductive system. It is sometimes difficult to identify this coercion because other forms of abuse are often occurring simultaneously.

Reproductive coercion can be exerted in many ways:

- Refusing to use a condom or other type of birth control
- Breaking or removing a condom during intercourse

- Lying about their methods of birth control (ex. lying about having a vasectomy, lying about being on the pill)
- Refusing to "pull out" if that is the agreed upon method of birth control
- Forcing you to not use any birth control (ex. the pill, condom, shot, ring, etc.)
- Removing birth control methods (ex. rings, IUDs, contraceptive patches)
- Sabotaging birth control methods (ex. poking holes in condoms, tampering with pills or flushing them down the toilet)
- Withholding finances needed to purchase birth control
- Monitoring your menstrual cycles
- Forcing pregnancy and not supporting your decision about when or if you want to have a child
- Forcing you to get an abortion, or preventing you from getting one
- Threatening you or acting violent if you don't comply with their wishes to either end or continue a pregnancy
- Continually keeping you pregnant (getting you pregnant again shortly after you give birth)

Reproductive coercion can also come in the form of pressure, guilt and shame from an abusive partner. Some examples are if your abusive partner is constantly talking about having children or making you feel guilty for not having or wanting children with them — especially if you already have kids with someone else.

Financial Abuse

Economic or financial abuse is when an abusive partner extends their power and control into the area of finances. This abuse can take different forms, including an abusive partner:

- Giving an allowance and closely watching how you spend it or demanding receipts for purchases
- Placing your pay check in their bank account and denying you access to it
- Preventing you from viewing or having access to bank accounts
- Forbidding you to work or limiting the hours that you can work

- Maxing out credit cards in your name without permission or not paying the bills on credit cards, which could ruin your credit score
- Stealing money from you or your family and friends
- Using funds from children's savings accounts without your permission
- Living in your home but refusing to work or contribute to the household
- Making you give them your tax returns or confiscating joint tax returns
- Refusing to give you money to pay for necessities/shared expenses like food, clothing, transportation, or medical care and medicine.

Digital Abuse

Digital abuse is the use of technologies such as texting and social networking to bully, harass, stalk or intimidate a partner. Often this behavior is a form of verbal or emotional abuse perpetrated online. You may be experiencing digital abuse if your partner:

- Tells you who you can or can't be friends with on Facebook and other sites.
- Sends you negative, insulting or even threatening emails, Facebook messages, tweets, DMs or other messages online.
- Uses sites like Facebook, Twitter, foursquare and others to keep constant tabs on you.
- Puts you down in their status updates.
- Sends you unwanted, explicit pictures and demands you send some in return.
- Pressures you to send explicit videos.
- Steals or insists on being given your passwords.
- Constantly texts you and makes you feel like you can't be separated from your phone for fear that you will be punished.
- Looks through your phone frequently, checks up on your pictures, texts and outgoing calls.
- Tags you unkindly in pictures on Instagram, Tumblr, etc.

- Uses any kind of technology (such <u>spyware</u> or GPS in a car or on a phone) to monitor you

You never deserve to be mistreated, online or off. Remember:

- Your partner should respect your relationship boundaries.
- It is ok to turn off your phone. You have the right to be alone and spend time with friends and family without your partner getting angry.
- You do not have to text any pictures or statements that you are uncomfortable sending, especially nude or partially nude photos, known as "sexting."
- You lose control of any electronic message once your partner receives it. They may forward it, so don't send anything you fear could be seen by others.
- You do not have to share your passwords with anyone.
- Know your privacy settings. Social networks such as Facebook allow the user to control how their information is shared and who has access to it. These are often customizable and are found in the privacy section of the site. Remember, registering for some applications (apps) require you to change your privacy settings.
- Be mindful when using check-ins like Facebook Places and foursquare. Letting an abusive partner know where you are could be dangerous. Also, always ask your friends if it's ok for you to check them in. You never know if they are trying to keep their location secret. You have the right to feel comfortable and safe in your relationship, even online.

Safety Plans

- Identify your partner's use and level of force so that you can assess the risk of physical danger to you and your children before it occurs.
- Identify safe areas of the house where there are no weapons and there are ways to escape. If arguments occur, try to move to those areas.
- Don't run to where the children are, as your partner may hurt them as well.

- If violence is unavoidable, make yourself a small target. Dive into a corner and curl up into a ball with your face protected and arms around each side of your head, fingers entwined.
- If possible, have a phone accessible at all times and know what numbers to call for help. Know where the nearest public phone is located. Know the phone number to your local shelter. If your life is in danger, call the police.
- Let trusted friends and neighbors know of your situation and develop a plan and visual signal for when you need help.
- Teach your children how to get help. Instruct them not to get involved in the violence between you and your partner. Plan a code word to signal to them that they should get help or leave the house.
- Tell your children that violence is never right, even when someone they love is being violent. Tell them that neither you, nor they, are at fault or are the cause of the violence, and that when anyone is being violent, it is important to stay safe.
- Practice how to get out safely. Practice with your children.
- Plan for what you will do if your children tells your partner of your plan or if your partner otherwise finds out about your plan.
- Keep weapons like guns and knives locked away and as inaccessible as possible.
- Make a habit of backing the car into the driveway and keeping it fueled. Keep the driver's door unlocked and others locked — for a quick escape.
- Try not to wear scarves or long jewelry that could be used to strangle you.
- Create several plausible reasons for leaving the house at different times of the day or night.

"Why Don't They Just Leave?"

People who have never been abused often wonder why a person wouldn't just leave an abusive relationship. They don't understand that leaving can be more complicated than it seems.

Leaving is often the most dangerous time for a victim of abuse, because abuse is about power and control. When a victim leaves, they are taking control and threatening the abusive partner's power, which could cause the abusive partner to retaliate in very destructive ways.

Aside from this danger, there are many reasons why people stay in abusive relationships. Here are just a few of the common ones:

- **Fear:** A person may be afraid of what will happen if they decide to leave the relationship.
- **Believing Abuse is Normal:** A person may not know what a healthy relationship looks like, perhaps from growing up in an environment where abuse was common, and they may not recognize that their relationship is unhealthy.
- **Fear of Being Outed:** If someone is in an LGBTQ relationship and has not yet come out to everyone, their partner may threaten to reveal this secret.
- **Embarrassment or Shame:** It's often difficult for someone to admit that they've been abused. They may feel they've done something wrong by becoming involved with an abusive partner. They may also worry that their friends and family will judge them.
- **Low Self-Esteem:** When an abusive partner constantly puts someone down and blames them for the abuse, it can be easy for the victim to believe those statements and think that the abuse is their fault.
- **Love:** So often, the victim feels love for their abusive partner. They may have children with them and want to maintain their family. Abusive people can often be charming, especially at the beginning of a relationship, and the victim may hope that their partner will go back to being that person. They may only want the violence to stop, not for the relationship to end entirely.

Leaving a Relationship

Preparing to leave a relationship

Because violence could escalate when someone tries to leave, here are some things to keep in mind before you leave:

- Keep any evidence of physical abuse, such as pictures of injuries.
- Keep a journal of all violent incidences, noting dates, events and threats made, if possible. Keep your journal in a safe place.

- Know where you can go to get help. Tell someone what is happening to you.
- If you are injured, go to a doctor or an emergency room and report what happened to you. Ask that they document your visit.
- Plan with your children and identify a safe place for them, like a room with a lock or a friend's house where they can go for help. Reassure them that their job is to stay safe, not to protect you.
- Contact your local shelter and find out about laws and other resources available to you before you have to use them during a crisis. WomensLaw.org has state by state legal information.
- Acquire job skills or take courses at a community college as you can.
- Try to set money aside or ask friends or family members to hold money for you.

When you leave

Make a plan for how and where you will escape quickly. You may request a police escort or stand-by when you leave. If you have to leave in a hurry, use the following list of items as a guide to what you need to bring with you. Our advocates can help you come up with a personalized safety plan for leaving.

1) Identification

- Driver's license
- Birth certificate and children's birth certificates
- Social security cards
- Financial information
- Money and/or credit cards (in your name)
- Checking and/or savings account books

2) Legal Papers

- Protective order
- Copies of any lease or rental agreements, or the deed to your home
- Car registration and insurance papers
- Health and life insurance papers
- Medical records for you and your children

- School records
- Work permits/green Card/visa
- Passport
- Divorce and custody papers
- Marriage license

3) Emergency Numbers

- Your local police and/or sheriff's department
- Your local domestic violence program or shelter
- Friends, relatives and family members
- Your local doctor's office and hospital
- County and/or District Attorney's Office

4) Other

- Medications
- Extra set of house and car keys
- Valuable jewelry
- Pay-as-you-go cell phone
- Address book
- Pictures and sentimental items
- Several changes of clothes for you and your children
- Emergency money

After you Leave

Your safety plan should include ways to ensure your continued safety after leaving an abusive relationship. Here are some safety precautions to consider:

- Change your locks and phone number.

- Call the telephone company to request caller ID. Ask that your phone number be blocked so that if you call anyone, neither your partner nor anyone else will be able to get your new, unlisted phone number.
- Change your work hours and the route you take to work.
- Change the route taken to transport children to school or consider changing your children's schools.
- Alert school authorities of the situation.
- If you have a restraining order, keep a certified copy of it with you at all times, and inform friends, neighbors and employers that you have a restraining order in effect.
- Call law enforcement to enforce the order and give copies of the restraining order to employers, neighbors and schools along with a picture of the offender.
- Consider renting a post office box or using the address of a friend for your mail (be aware that addresses are on restraining orders and police reports, and be careful to whom you give your new address and phone number).
- Reschedule appointments that the offender is aware of.
- Use different stores and frequent different social spots.
- Alert neighbors and request that they call the police if they feel you may be in danger.
- Replace wooden doors with steel or metal doors. Install security systems if possible.
- Install a motion sensitive lighting system.
- Tell people you work with about the situation and have your calls screened by one receptionist if possible.
- Tell people who take care of your children or drive them/pick them up from school and activities. Explain your situation to them and provide them with a copy of the restraining order.

- **Cultural/Religious Reasons:** Traditional gender roles supported by someone's culture or religion may influence them to stay rather than end the relationship for fear of bringing shame upon their family.
- **Language Barriers/Immigration Status:** If a person is undocumented, they may fear that reporting the abuse will affect their immigration status. Also, if their first language isn't English, it can be difficult to express the depth of their situation to others.

- **Lack of Money/Resources:** <u>Financial abuse</u> is common, and a victim may be financially dependent on their abusive partner. Without money, access to resources or even a place to go, it can seem impossible for them to leave the relationship. This feeling of helplessness can be especially strong if the person lives with their abusive partner.
- **Disability:** When someone is physically dependent on their abusive partner, they can feel that their well-being is connected to the relationship. This dependency could heavily influence their decision to stay in an abusive relationship.

Domestic Violence Contact Information by State

(Note: Each contact listed has been individually verified as correct at the time of print 10/2019)

Arizona Coalition to End Sexual and Domestic Violence

2800 N. Central Avenue, Suite 1570
Phoenix, AZ 85004
(602) 279-2900 Fax: (844) 252-3094
(800) 782-6400 Nationwide
Website: www.acesdv.org
Email: info@acesdv.org

Arkansas Coalition Against Domestic Violence

700 S. Rock Street

Little Rock, AR 72202

(501) 907-5612 Fax: (501) 907-5618

(800) 269-4668 Nationwide

Website: www.domesticpeace.com

Email: acadv@domesticpeace.com

California Partnership to End Domestic Violence

1107 9th Street, #910

Sacramento, CA 95812

(916) 444-7163 Fax: (916) 444-7165

(800) 524-4765 Nationwide

Website: www.cpedv.org

Email: info@cpedv.org

Colorado Coalition Against Domestic Violence

1330 Fox Street, Suite 3

PO Box 40328

Denver, CO 80203

(303) 831-9632 Fax: (303) 832-7067

(888) 778-7091

Website: www.ccadv.org

Email: info@ccadv.org

Connecticut Coalition Against Domestic Violence

912 Silas Deane Highway, Lower Level

Wethersfield, CT 06109

(860) 282-7899 Fax: (860) 282-7892

(888) 774-2900 In State DV Hotline

Website: www.ctcadv.org

Email: contactus@ctcadv.org

Delaware Coalition Against Domestic Violence

100 West 10th Street, Suite 903

Wilmington, DE 19801

(302) 658-2958 Fax: (302) 658-5049

(800) 701-0456 Statewide

Website: www.dcadv.org

Email: dcadvadmin@dcadv.org

DC Coalition Against Domestic Violence

5 Thomas Circle Northwest

Washington, DC 20005

(202) 299-1181 Fax: (202) 299-1193

Website: www.dccadv.org

Email: info@dccadv.org

Florida Coalition Against Domestic Violence

425 Office Plaza Drive

Tallahassee, FL 32301

(850) 425-2749 Fax: (850) 425-3091

(850) 621-4202 TDD

(800) 500-1119 In State

Website: www.fcadv.org

Georgia Coalition Against Domestic Violence

114 New Street, Suite B

Decatur, GA 30030

(404) 209-0280 Fax: (404) 766-3800

(800) 334-2836 Crisis Line

Website: www.gcadv.org

Email: info@gcadv.org

Hawaii State Coalition Against Domestic Violence

1164 Bishop Street, Suite 1609

Honolulu, HI 96813

(808) 832-9316 Fax: (808) 841-6028

Website: www.hscadv.org

Email: admin@hscadv.org

Idaho Coalition Against Sexual and Domestic Violence

Linen Building

1402 W. Grove Street

Boise, ID 83702

(208) 384-0419 Fax: (208) 331-0687

(888) 293-6118 Nationwide

Website: www.idvsa.org

Email: info@engagingvoices.org

Illinois Coalition Against Domestic Violence

806 South College Street

Springfield, IL 62704

(217) 789-2830 Fax: (217) 789-1939

(217) 242-0376 TTY

Website: www.ilcadv.org

Email: ilcadv@ilcadv.org

Indiana Coalition Against Domestic Violence

1915 West 18th Street, Suite B

Indianapolis, IN 46202

(317) 917-3685 Fax: (317) 917-3695

(800) 332-7385 In State

Website:www.icadvinc.org

Email: icadv@icadvinc.org

Iowa Coalition Against Domestic Violence

6200 Aurora Avenue, Suite 405E

Urbandale, IA 50322

(515) 244-8028 Fax: (515) 244-7417

(800) 942-0333 In State Hotline

Website: www.icadv.org

Email: icadv@icadv.org

Kansas Coalition Against Sexual and Domestic Violence

634 Southwest Harrison Street

Topeka, KS 66603

(785) 232-9784 Fax: (785) 266-1874

Website: www.kcsdv.org

Email: coalition@kcsdv.org

Kentucky Domestic Violence Association

111 Darby Shire Circle

Frankfort, KY 40601

(502) 209-5382 Phone Fax (502) 226-5382

Website: www.kdva.org

Email: info@kdva.org

Louisiana Coalition Against Domestic Violence

P.O. Box 77308

Baton Rouge, LA 70879

(225) 752-1296 Fax: (225) 751-8927

Website: www.lcadv.org

Email: info@lcadv.org

Maine Coalition to End Domestic Violence

One Weston Court, Box #2

Augusta, ME 04330

(207) 430-8334 Fax: (207) 430-8348

Website: www.mcedv.org

Email: info@MCADV.org

Maryland Network Against Domestic Violence

4601 Presidents Drive, Suite 370

Lanham, MD 20706

(301) 429-3601 Fax: (301) 809-0422

(800) 634-3577 Nationwide

Website: www.mnadv.org

Email: info@mnadv.org

Jane Doe, Inc./Massachusetts Coalition Against Sexual Assault and Domestic Violence

14 Beacon Street, Suite 507

Boston, MA 02108

(617) 248-0922 Fax: (617) 248-0902

(617) 263-2200 TTY/TDD

Website: www.janedoe.org

Email: info@janedoe.org

Michigan Coalition Against Domestic and Sexual Violence

3893 Okemos Road, Suite B-2

Okemos, MI 48864

(517) 347-7000 Phone/TTY Fax: (517) 248-0902

Website: www.mcedsv.org

Email: general@mcedsv.org

Minnesota Coalition For Battered Women

60 E. Plato Blvd., Suite 130

St. Paul, MN 55107

(651) 646-6177 Fax: (651) 646-1527

(651) 646-0994 Crisis Line

(800) 289-6177 Nationwide

Website: www.mcbw.org

Email: mcbw@mcbw.org

Mississippi Coalition Against Domestic Violence

P.O. Box 4703

Jackson, MS 39296

(601) 981-9196 Fax: (601) 981-2501

(800) 898-3234

Website: www.mcadv.org

Email: support@mcadv.org

Missouri Coalition Against Domestic and Sexual Violence

217 Oscar Drive, Suite A

Jefferson City, MO 65101

(573) 634-4161 Fax: (573) 636-3728

Website: www.mocadsv.org

Email: mocadsv@mocadsv.org

Montana Coalition Against Domestic & Sexual Violence

P.O. Box 818

Helena, MT 59624

(406) 443-7794 Fax: (406) 443-7818

(888) 404-7794 Nationwide

Website: www.mcadsv.com

Email: mtcoalition@mcadsv.com

Nebraska Domestic Violence Sexual Assault Coalition

245 S. 84th Street, Suite 200

Lincoln, NE 68510

(402) 476-6256 Fax: (402) 476-6806

(800) 876-6238 In State Hotline

(877) 215-0167 Spanish Hotline

Website: www.ndvsac.org

Email: help@ndvsac.org

Nevada Network Against Domestic Violence

250 South Rock BLVD., Suite 116

Reno, NV 89502

(775) 828-1115 Fax: (775) 828-9911

Website: www.nnadv.org

Email: info@nnadv.org

New Hampshire Coalition Against Domestic and Sexual Violence

P.O. Box 353

Concord, NH 03302

(603) 224-8893 Fax: (603) 228-6096

(866) 644-3574 In State

Website: www.nhcadsv.org

Email: info@nhcadsv.org

New Jersey Coalition for Battered Women

1670 Whitehorse Hamilton Square Road

Trenton, NJ 08690

(609) 584-8107 Fax: (609) 584-9750

(800) 572-7233 In State

Website: www.njcbw.org

Email: info@njcbw.org

New Mexico Coalition Against Domestic Violence

1210 Luisa Street, Suite 7

Mailing Address: 1000 Cordova Place, #52

Santa Fe, NM 87505

(505) 246-9240 Fax: (505) 246-9434

(800) 773-3645 In State

Website: www.nmcadv.org

Email: info@nmcadv.org

New York State Coalition Against Domestic Violence

119 Washington Avenue, Suite 12210

Albany, NY 12054

(518) 482-5464 Fax: (518) 482-3807

(800) 942-5465 English-In State

(800) 942-6908 Spanish-In State

Website: www.nyscadv.org

Email: nyscadv@nyscadv.org

North Carolina Coalition Against Domestic Violence

3710 University Drive, Suite 140

Durham, NC 27707

(919) 956-9124 Fax: (919) 682-1449

(888) 997-9124

Website: www.nccadv.org

North Dakota Council on Abused Women's Services

521 E. Main Avenue, Suite 250

Bismarck, ND 58501

(701) 255-6240 Fax: (701) 255-1904

(888) 255-6240 Nationwide

Website: www.ndcaws.org

Email: contact@cawsnorthdakota.org

Action Ohio Coalition For Battered Women

P.O. Box 423

Worthington, OH 43085

(614) 825-0551 Fax: (614) 825-0673

(888) 622-9315 In State

Website: www.actionohio.org

Email: actionohio@wowway.biz

Ohio Domestic Violence Network

1855 E. Dublin Granville Road

Columbus, OH 43229

(614) 781-9651 Fax: (614) 781-9652

(614) 781-9654 TTY

(800) 934-9840

Website: www.odvn.org

Email: info@odvn.org

Oklahoma Coalition Against Domestic Violence and Sexual Assault

3815 North Santa Fe Avenue, Suite 124

Oklahoma City, OK 73118

(405) 524-0700 Fax: (405) 524-0711

Website: www.ocadvsa.org

Email: Prevention@ocadvsa.org

Oregon Coalition Against Domestic and Sexual Violence

9570 SW Barbur Boulevard, Suite 214

Portland, OR 97219

(503) 230-1951 Fax: (503) 230-1973

(877) 230-1951

Website: www.ocadsv.com

Email: adminasst@ocadsv.com

Pennsylvania Coalition Against Domestic Violence

3605 Vartan Way, Suite 101

Harrisburg, PA 17110

(717) 545-6400 Fax: (717) 545-9456

(800) 932-4632 Nationwide

Website: www.pcadv.org

The Office of Women Advocates

Box 11382

Fernandez Juancus Station

Santurce, PR 00910

(787) 721-7676 Fax: (787) 725-9248

Rhode Island Coalition Against Domestic Violence

422 Post Road, Suite 102

Warwick, RI 02888

(401) 467-9940 Fax: (401) 467-9943

(800) 494-8100 In State

Website: www.ricadv.org

Email: ricadv@ricadv.org

South Carolina Coalition Against Domestic Violence and Sexual Assault

P.O. Box 7776

Columbia, SC 29202

(803) 256-2900 Fax: (803) 256-1030

(800) 260-9293 Nationwide

Website: www.sccadvasa.org

South Dakota Coalition Against Domestic Violence & Sexual Assault

P.O. Box 141

Pierre, SD 57501

(605) 945-0869 Fax: (605) 945-0870

(800) 572-9196 Nationwide

Website: www.sdcedsv.org

Email: SKing@SDCEDSV.org

Tennessee Coalition Against Domestic and Sexual Violence

2 International Plaza Drive, Suite 425

Nashville, TN 37217

(615) 386-9406 Fax: (615) 383-2967

(800) 289-9018 In State

Website: www.tncoalition.org

Email: tcadsv@tcadsv.org

Texas Council on Family Violence

P.O. Box 163865

Austin, TX 78716

(512) 794-1133 Fax: (512) 794-1199

Website: www.tcfv.org

Utah Domestic Violence Coalition

124 South 400 East, Suite 300

Salt Lake City, UT 84111

(801) 521-5544 Fax: (801) 521-5548

Website: www.udvc.org

Women's Coalition of St. Croix

P.O. Box 222734

Christiansted

St. Croix, VI 00822

(340) 773-9272 Fax: (340) 773-9062

Website: www.wcstx.org

Email: info@wcstx.org

Vermont Network Against Domestic Violence and Sexual Assault

P.O. Box 405

Montpelier, VT 05601

(802) 223-1302 Fax: (802) 223-6943

(802) 223-1115 TTY

Website: www.vtnetwork.org

Email: vtnetwork@vtnetwork.org

Virginia Sexual & Domestic Violence Action Alliance

1118 West Main Street

Richmond, VA 23230

Office: 804.377.0335 Fax: 804.377.0339

Website: www.vsdvalliance.org

E-mail: info@vsdvalliance.org

Washington State Coalition Against Domestic Violence

711 Capitol Way, Suite 702

Olympia, WA 98501

(360) 586-1022 Fax: (360) 586-1024

(360) 586-1029 TTY

1511 Third Avenue, Suite 433

Seattle, WA 98101

(206) 389-2515 Fax: (206) 389-2520

(800) 886-2880 In State

(206) 389-2900 TTY

Website: www.wscadv.org

Email: wscadv@wscadv.org

Washington State Native American Coalition Against Domestic and Sexual Assault

P.O. Box 3937

Sequim, WA 98382

(360) 352-3120 Fax: (360) 357-3858

(888) 352-3120

Website: www.womenspirit.net

West Virginia Coalition Against Domestic Violence

5004 Elk River Road South

Elkview, WV 25071

(304) 965-3552 Fax: (304) 965-3572

Website: www.wvcadv.org

Email: website@wvcadv.org

End Domestic Abuse Wisconsin: The Wisconsin Coalition Against Domestic Violence

1245 East Washington Avenue, Suite 150

Madison, WI 53703

(608) 255-0539 Fax: (608) 255-3560

Website: www.endabusewi.org

Email: wcadv@wcadv.org

Wyoming Coalition Against Domestic Violence and Sexual Assault

P.O. Box 236

710 Garfield Street, Suite 218

Laramie, WY 82073

(307) 755-5481 Fax: (307) 755-5482

(800) 990-3877 Nationwide

Website: www.wyomingdvsa.org

Email: info@wyomingdvsa.org

Phone Numbers to Call for Confidential Help:
US National Domestic Violence

Hotline: **1−800−799−SAFE (7233)** or **TTY 1−800−787−3224**

Canadian National Domestic Violence Hotline: **1-800-363-9010**

UK Domestic Violence Hotline: **0808 2000 247**

Verizon Wireless customers

You are able to connect to the National Domestic Violence Hotline simply by dialing #Hope on your mobile phone.

$\mathscr{S}$cripture References

Healing Verses from Psalms

The Book of Psalms is a collection of cries, prayers and praise. The authors of each chapter experienced every struggle, heartache and fear imaginable. This collection of comforting verses will help guide you toward whole and complete healing.

- "Then they cried to the LORD in their trouble, and he saved them from their distress. He sent out his word and healed them; he rescued them from the grave. Let them give thanks to the LORD for his unfailing love and his wonderful deeds for mankind." ~ **Psalms 107:19-21**

  "LORD my God, I called to you for help, and you healed me." ~ **Psalms 30:2**

- "The righteous cry out, and the LORD hears them; he delivers them from all their troubles. The LORD is close to the broken-hearted and saves those who are crushed in spirit. The righteous person may have many troubles, but the LORD delivers him from them all; he protects all his bones, not one of them will be broken. Evil will slay the wicked; the foes of the righteous will be condemned. The LORD will rescue his servants; no one who takes refuge in him will be condemned." ~ **Psalms 34:17-22**

- "Praise the LORD, my soul, and forget not all his benefits - who forgives all your sins and heals all your diseases, who redeems your life from the pit and crowns you with love and compassion." ~ **Psalms 103:2-4**

- "Have mercy on me, LORD, for I am faint; heal me, LORD, for my bones are in agony." ~ **Psalms 6:2**

- "The LORD protects and preserves them— they are counted among the blessed in the land - he does not give them over to the desire of their foes. The LORD sustains them on their sickbed and restores them from their bed of illness." ~ **Psalms 41:2-3**

- "I said, "Have mercy on me, LORD; heal me, for I have sinned against you." ~ **Psalms 41:4**

- "He heals the broken hearted and binds up their wounds." ~ **Psalms 147:3**

- "The LORD is my shepherd, I lack nothing. He makes me lie down in green pastures, he leads me beside quiet waters, he refreshes my soul. He guides me along the right paths for his name's sake. Even though I walk through the darkest valley, I will fear no evil, for you are with me; your rod and your staff, they comfort me. You prepare a table before me in the presence of my enemies. You anoint my head with oil; my cup overflows. Surely your goodness and love will follow me all the days of my life, and I will dwell in the house of the LORD forever." ~ **Psalms 23**

- "Hear, LORD, and be merciful to me; LORD, be my help." You turned my wailing into dancing; you removed my sackcloth and clothed me with joy" ~ **Psalms 30:10-11**

- "My flesh and my heart may fail, but God is the strength of my heart and my portion forever." ~ **Psalms 73:26**

Domestic Violence Is Sinful.

"The acts of the flesh are obvious: sexual immorality, impurity and debauchery; idolatry and witchcraft; hatred, discord, jealousy, fits of rage, selfish ambition, dissensions, factions and envy; drunkenness, orgies, and the like. I warn you, as I did before, that those who live like this will not inherit the kingdom of God." (Galatians 5:19-21)

"Do not lie. Do not deceive one another." (Leviticus 19:11)

"The Lord examines both the righteous and the wicked. He hates those who love violence. He will rain down blazing coals and burning sulfur on the wicked, punishing them with scorching winds." (Psalm 11:5–7, NLT)

"They are always twisting what I say; they spend their days to harm me." (Psalm 56:5, NLT)

"Therefore, pride is their necklace. They clothe themselves with violence." (Psalm 73:6)

"A scoundrel and villain, who goes about with a corrupt mouth, who winks with his eye, signals with his feet and motions with his fingers, who plots evil with deceit in his heart—he always stirs up dissension. Therefore, disaster will overtake him in an instant; he will suddenly be destroyed without remedy." (Proverbs 6:12–15)

"Here are six things God hates, and one more that he loathes with a passion: eyes that are arrogant, a tongue that lies, hands that murder the innocent, a heart that hatches evil plots, feet that race down a wicked track, a mouth that lies under oath, a troublemaker in the family." (Proverbs 6:16)

The Lord detests all the proud of heart. Be sure of this: They will not go unpunished. (Proverbs 15:5)

A worthless man plots evil, and his speech is like a scorching fire. A dishonest man spreads strife, and a whisperer separates close friends. A man of violence entices his neighbor and leads him in a way that is not good. (Proverbs 16:27-29)

Do you see a person wise in their own eyes? There is more hope for a fool than for them. (Proverbs 26:12)

Like a madman shooting firebrands or deadly arrows is a man who deceives his neighbour and says, "I was only joking!" (Proverbs 26:18–19)

A malicious man disguises himself with his lips, but in his heart, he harbours deceit. Though his speech is charming, do not believe him, for seven abominations fill his heart. His malice may be concealed by deception, but his wickedness will be exposed in the assembly. (Proverbs 26:24–26)

Your fasting ends in quarrelling and strife, and in striking each other with wicked fists. You cannot fast as you do today and expect your voice to be heard on high. (Isaiah 58:4)

"For I hate divorce," says the Lord, the God of Israel. "And I hate the man who does wrong to his wife," says the Lord of All. "So be careful in your spirit and be one who can be trusted." (Malachi 2:16)

"You're familiar with the command to the ancients, "Do not murder." I'm telling you that anyone who is so much as angry with a brother or sister is guilty of murder. Carelessly call a brother "idiot!" and you just might find yourself hauled into court. Thoughtlessly yell "stupid!" at a sister and you are on the brink of hellfire. The simple moral fact is that words kill. "(Matthew 5:21–22, The Message)

"Love is patient, love is kind. It does not envy, it does not boast, it is not proud. It does not dishonor others, it is not self-seeking, it is not easily angered, it keeps no record of wrongs." (1 Corinthians 13:4-5)

"Do not let any unwholesome talk come out of your mouths, but only what is helpful for building others up according to their needs, that it may benefit those who listen." (Ephesians 4:29)

"Nor should there be obscenity, foolish talk or coarse joking, which are out of place…" (Ephesians 5:4)

"If you claim to be religious but don't control your tongue, you are fooling yourself, and your religion is worthless." (James 1:26, NLT)

Abusers Look Pleasing to those Outside the Home Because They Usually Only Abuse While Inside the Home. It is often hard for us to believe a "Good Christian" could abuse. But God is not surprised.

"But the Lord said to Samuel, "Do not consider his appearance or his height, for I have rejected him. The Lord does not look at the things people look at. People look at the outward appearance, but the Lord looks at the heart." (1 Samuel 16:7)

"Watch out for false prophets. They come to you in sheep's clothing, but inwardly they are ferocious wolves. By their fruit you will recognize them. Do people pick grapes from thorn bushes or figs from thistles? Likewise, every good tree bears good fruit, but a bad tree bears bad fruit. A good tree cannot bear bad fruit, and a bad tree cannot bear good fruit. Every tree that does not bear good fruit is cut down and thrown into the fire. Thus, by their fruit you will recognize them." (Matthew 7:15-20)

Separating from the unrepentant: The Bible supports the idea of limiting togetherness for the sake of "binding evil."

"Turn from evil and do good; then you will dwell in the land forever." (Psalm 37:27)

"Let not my heart be drawn to what is evil, to take part in wicked deeds with men who are evildoers; let me not eat of their delicacies. Keep me from the snares they have laid for me, from the traps set by evildoers. Let the wicked fall into their own nets, while I pass by in safety." (Psalm 141:4, 9-10)

"They rejected my advice and paid no attention when I corrected them. Therefore, they must eat the bitter fruit of living their own way, choking on their own schemes" (Proverbs 1:30)

"Go from the presence of a foolish man, when you do not perceive in him the lips of knowledge." (Proverbs 14:7)

"The prudent see danger and take refuge, but the simple keep going and pay the penalty." (Proverbs 27:12)

"When they had gone, an angel of the Lord appeared to Joseph in a dream. "Get up," he said, "take the child and his mother and escape to Egypt. Stay there until I tell you, for Herod is going to search for the child to kill him." So, he got up, took the child and his mother during the night and left for Egypt". (Matthew 2:13-14)

"When you are persecuted in one place, flee to another." (Matthew 10:23)

"If your brother or sister sins, go and point out their fault, just between the two of you. If they listen to you, you have won them over. But if they will not listen, take one or two others along, so that 'every matter may be established by the testimony of two or three witnesses. If they still refuse to listen, tell it to the church; and if they refuse to listen even to the church, treat them as you would a pagan or a tax collector." (Matthew 18:15–17)

"But now I am writing to you that you must not associate with anyone who claims to be a brother or sister but is sexually immoral or greedy, an idolater or slanderer, a drunkard or swindler. Do not even eat with such people. . . Expel the wicked person from among you." (1 Corinthians 5:11, 13)

"Take no part in the unfruitful works of darkness, but instead expose them." (Ephesians 5:11)

"People will be lovers of themselves, lovers of money, boastful, proud, abusive, disobedient to their parents, ungrateful, unholy, without love, unforgiving, slanderous, without self-control, brutal, not lovers of the good, treacherous, rash, conceited, lovers of pleasure rather than lovers of God— having a form of godliness but denying its power. Have nothing to do with such people." (2 Timothy 3:2-5)

Abuse victims are often told to submit to the abusive behaviour of their spouses. This is an unfortunate occurrence in churches and synagogues.

In 1 Samuel chapter 25, we see the story of Abigail and her husband Nabal. When Abigail's fool of a husband speaks abusively to David and David is about to slaughter him and every male in his household, Abigail comes to the rescue. She doesn't "submit" to her foolish husband. Instead, rather than following Nabal's irrational wishes, she decides to protect her household.

In 1 Samuel chapters 18 through 31, in spite of God's general instructions to submit to the laws of the land and to higher authorities, when David feared for his life because of King Saul's jealous rages, God didn't instruct David to "submit to the King and trust me to take care of you." Instead, David fled, always respecting the position of King Saul, but not allowing himself to be abused by him.

What Does the Bible Say About Divorce for Abuse?

1. Many Christians believe there are only two valid reasons given for divorce in the Bible: adultery (Matthew 5:31-32), and desertion by an unbeliever, (1 Corinthians 7:1-16). Both of these reasons come from the New Testament. However, 2 Timothy 3:16-17 says: All Scripture is God-breathed and is useful for teaching, rebuking, correcting and training in righteousness, so that the servant of God may be thoroughly equipped for every good work.

2. In his booklet God's Protection of Women: When Abuse is Worse than Divorce, 1 Herb Vander Lugt, author and senior research editor for RBC Ministries explains how Jesus and the Apostle Paul both knew the Old Testament completely, and their comments were

meant to add to, rather than replace or change what was already said in the Old Testament about marriage and divorce.

In Matthew 5:31-32 and Matthew 19:1-9, Jesus was not giving a full treatise on divorce law, and he was not responding to abused women. Instead, in Matthew 5 He was focusing on hard-hearted men who were "adulterizing" their wives, and in Matthew 19, He was responding to self-righteous Pharisees who were trying to pit Jesus's words against those of Moses.

3. The Old Testament prescribed laws for Israelite women who were sold for the purpose of marriage, and foreign women taken as captives during war. Both these groups of women were allowed to "go free" (divorce) if it were possible they were going to be mistreated, i.e. abused (Exodus 21:7-11 and Deuteronomy 21:10-14).

4. Many Christians say God "hates divorce," and therefore, victims of abuse should never divorce. **God said He hated the <u>specific</u> divorces in Malachi 2:10 – 16**, where Israelite men were divorcing the godly Israelite wives they had married in their youth and were marrying instead the idol worshiping women of surrounding tribes.

5. Though God hates divorce, He required the Israelite men to divorce their pagan, idol worshiping wives in order not to defile the people of Israel, (Ezra 9 – 10).

6. Throughout the gospels, Jesus showed how He is more concerned with the intent of the law than He is about the letter of the law.

(1 Taken and adapted from God's Protection of Women, When Abuse is Worse than Divorce by Herb Vander Lugt, Copyright 2005 by RBC Ministries, Grand Rapids, MI. Used by permission. All rights reserved.)

Journal Notes

Journal Notes

Journal Notes

Journal Notes

Journal Notes

_____

_____

_____

_____

_____

_____

_____

_____

_____

_____

_____

_____

_____

_____

_____

_____

_____

_____

_____

Journal Notes

Journal Notes

_____

_____

_____

_____

_____

_____

_____

_____

_____

_____

_____

_____

_____

_____

_____

_____

Journal Notes

Journal Notes

Journal Notes

Journal Notes

Journal Notes

Journal Notes

Journal Notes

Journal Notes

_____

_____

_____

_____

_____

_____

_____

_____

_____

_____

_____

_____

_____

_____

_____

_____

_____

_____

Journal Notes

Journal Notes

Journal Notes

Journal Notes

Journal Notes

Journal Notes

_____

_____

_____

_____

_____

_____

_____

_____

_____

_____

_____

_____

_____

_____

_____

_____

_____

_____

Journal Notes

Journal Notes

Journal Notes

Journal Notes

Journal Notes

ABOUT THE AUTHOR

Evangelist Tanya R. Thompson is an African-American Christian Author. She is the mother of one daughter, Mikayla (Kayla) Thompson who is currently a Senior Interdisciplinary Studies major at Tennessee State University. She is the CEO and Founder of Glory After the Rain Ministries. Tanya presents a Facebook live Early Morning Devotional series on Facebook that attracts viewers from across the continent and other countries. In addition to this, she is pursuing a long-awaited dream of podcasting, which debuts December 2019. Evangelist Tanya travels the country spreading the message of Jesus Christ through Women's Conferences, Revivals, Talk Shows and Workshops. Starting October 2019, she will be offering a Beginners Writing course online for women who desire to birth their first book.

She currently holds a Bachelor of Divinity and an Associate Degree of Divinity from Christian Leaders Institute and Christian Leaders College in Grand Rapids, MI. She was ordained as a Deaconess and subsequently an ordained Minister through Pastor Henry Reyenga of Grand Rapids, Michigan. Tanya is currently pursuing a dual -enrolment program to obtain her Master and PhD in Theological studies. She has served as a guest Instructor for the RCPI Bible College in Kenya Africa. She is a proud member of the "More than a Woman Alliance" in Middle Tennessee where she serves as a Tier One Leader. Her true passion is the empowerment of women who have been affected by domestic violence. As a survivor of domestic violence, she is committed to speaking out and telling the story of those directly affected by this horrible epidemic.

About the Co-Author

Mikayla Thompson is an African-American Christian Author, Visual Artist and Illustrator. She is a Senior at Tennessee State University majoring in Interdisciplinary studies. Kayla is a member of the Tennessee State University Tiger Belles track team, where she is an award-winning member of the Throws team. She competes in hammer, weights, shot put and discus. She is also a member of the International Thespian Society for Actors and Actresses. Additionally, she is awaiting induction into the National Society of Leadership and Success. She is the CEO and creator of BLAC Beauty Cosmetics, which is an all-natural, personally formulated lip gloss line as well as distributor of 3D/4D/5D lashes. She also owns a personal line of hand-made candles and gifts.

Mikayla has a passion for community outreach with emphasis on homelessness initiatives and survivors of domestic violence. Kayla has illustrated one children's book and is currently working on a series of children's books to inspire and encourage young children across the globe. She enjoys speaking as a youth mentor to children across the nation.

For bookings contact Kayla Thompson at:
kayth81@gmail.com
blacbeautycosmetic@gmail.com

"I can do all things through Christ who strengthens me."
– Philippians 4:13

Please be sure to check out these other amazing titles released
by
Tanya R. Thompson

Each one is available on Amazon.com. Select titles will be coming to a Barnes Noble and Wal-Mart near you!

Straight from the Heart – A 30-day Devotional

Women Who Worship – A 30-day Devotional, full-color edition

Women Who Worship – A 30-day Devotional black and white edition

Redemption – available on Amazon.com

He Loves Me Not – in Digital and Soft Cover, Amazon.com

Silent Suffering, coming Spring 2020 to Amazon and Barnes-Noble

New! Bible Story Devotional Series, coming Summer 2020 to a Barnes & Noble, Amazon and Wal-Mart near you.

For booking inquiries please contact Glory After the Rain Ministries at:
gloryaftertherain@gmail.com

Made in the USA
Coppell, TX
08 March 2020